The Blackbirch
TREASURY OF
AMERICAN
POETRY

The Blackbirch
TREASURY OF
AMERICAN
POETRY

Severn River Media Center

BLACKBIRCH PRESS, INC.

WOODBRIDGE, CONNECTICUT

Published by Blackbirch Press, Inc.
260 Amity Road
Woodbridge, CT 06525

e-mail: staff@blackbirch.com
Web site: www.blackbirch.com

Material in this collection was compiled from:
Poetry for Young People/Carl Sandburg ©1995 Magnolia Editions Limited
Introduction ©1995 Frances Schoonmaker Bolin, Illustrations ©1995 Steven Arcells
Poetry for Young People/Edgar Allen Poe ©1995 Magnolia Editions Limited
Introduction ©1995 Brod Bagert, Illustrations ©1995 Carolynn Cobleigh
Poetry for Young People/Emily Dickinson ©1994 Magnolia Editions Limited
Introduction © Frances Schoonmaker Bolin, Illustrations ©1994 by Chi Chung
Poetry for Young People/Walt Whitman ©1997 Sterling Publishing Co., Inc.
Text ©1997 Jonathan Levin, Illustration ©1997 Jim Burke
Poetry for Young People/Robert Frost © Magnolia Editions Limited
Illustrations ©1994 Henri Sorensen
Poetry for Young People/Henry Wadsworth Longfellow ©1998 Sterling Publishing Co., Inc.
Introduction ©1998 Frances Schoonmaker, Illustrations ©1998 Chad Wallace

Photo credits and acknowledgments—see page 284

ISBN 1-56711-472-5

10 9 8 7 6 5 4 3 2 1

Printed in China

Library of Congress Cataloging-in-Publication Data Available

Contents

Carl Sandburg

Edited by Frances Schoonmaker Bolin
Illustrated by Steven Arcella

Restless as a Young Heart, Hunting

CARL SANDBURG WATCHED A THICK FOG MOVE FROM THE NEARBY Chicago harbor to settle over the park where he was walking. The year was 1913 and Sandburg, then a journalist for the *Chicago Daily News*, was on his way to interview a judge. Later, as he sat waiting in the judge's office, he pulled a piece of newspaper from his pocket. On it he wrote: "The fog comes on little cat feet, It sits looking over city and harbor on silent haunches and then moves on." (Look closely at page 8 to see how he revised it before it was published.) These few lines became one of his most famous poems.

When thirty-five-year-old Sandburg wrote "Fog," he had already published a small collection of poetry, but was not yet considered a great poet. Even though he had a steady job with the newspaper, he was restless, still trying to decide what to do with his life. Choosing a profession was no easy matter for him because he had so many interests and talents.

Born January 6, 1878, in Galesburg, Illinois, Sandburg was a wanderer who always wanted to try new things and go to new places. By age eighteen, he had held several jobs, including one delivering milk and another delivering blocks of ice to homes and stores. (This was before people had electric refrigerators.) He worked long, hard hours before and after school, and once nearly froze his feet walking four miles to and from the dairy without overshoes. There was no money for them; the twelve dollars a month Sandburg earned went to help his family.

The young Sandburg was not afraid of hard work, but he did not want to settle for work that was not interesting to him. His nose was always in a book, for his sixth grade teacher had told him, "You don't know what good friends books can be till you try them, till you try many of them." He liked to write, too, and his pockets were always full of odd scraps of paper on which he wrote his many ideas. He loved music and experimented with homemade musical instruments such as a willow whistle and a cigar-box banjo. (He once bought a banjo from a pawn shop for two dollars, and paid a quarter for three banjo lessons.) Most of all, Sandburg loved to travel.

For thirty-five years, Sandburg's father, August, worked as a blacksmith's helper for the Chicago, Burlington and Quincy Railroad (C.B. & Q.) ten hours a day, six days a week, with no vacations. His job was to beat hot iron into railroad parts. Sandburg's mother, Clara, worked to keep house for the family. August was serious, stern, and careful with the little money he earned. Clara was cheerful and full of life, and she valued learning. She once spent more than August could earn in a day to buy an encyclopedia for the children.

Both August and Clara came to the United States from Sweden and were proud of their heritage. Sandburg, the second of seven children (two of his younger brothers died when Carl was a teenager), spoke Swedish before he spoke English; but he wanted to be an American and was afraid that being Swedish meant that he was less American. By the time he reached second grade, he had convinced everyone, including his teachers, to call him Charlie instead of Carl. Not until many years later did he use the name Carl again, finally proud of being both Swedish and American.

Because his father worked for the C.B. & Q., Sandburg could get rail passes. When he was eighteen, his father let him take the train to Chicago alone. He walked all over the city, admiring its busy streets and the beautiful Lake Michigan. Little did he know then that Chicago, the powerful and exciting city he had always wanted to see, would become his home and the subject of many of his poems. However, after he came home, he did know that he would never be content to stay in one place and do monotonous work.

The following year Sandburg set out to see the West, becoming a hobo. For about five months he travelled across the United States—usually by train—and worked at odd jobs to support himself. He sang folk songs around a campfire with other hobos and slept under the stars. He worked in the wheat harvest in Kansas, washed dishes in Colorado, and passed up a chance to join the Gold Rush in Alaska. All the while he wrote in his journal, noting unusual bits of language, interesting faces, and the stories and songs of the people he met. He wrote about the many sights, sounds, and smells of the West, which later found their way into his poems. He read everything he could get his hands on, and he wrote about people, the earth, feelings, wishes, and thoughts. He began to experiment with writing many different forms of poetry. In one of his poems, "A Homely Winter Idyl" (see page 29), he tried writing like Emily Dickinson, using meter (a regular rhythm) and rhyme. But he most often returned to free verse, poetry without a predictable rhythm or rhyme.

"I got education in scraps and pieces of many kinds, not knowing they were part of my education," Sandburg wrote. He never went to high school because the family could only afford to send his older sister, Mary. But Mary shared her books with her brother, and he learned enough to be admitted to college. Though he studied hard and was a good student, Sandburg never graduated: instead of taking all the courses required for graduation, he only took classes in which he had an interest.

Sandburg grew up in the prairie country where Abraham Lincoln had lived. Throughout his life, Sandburg heard stories about Lincoln, many of which had never been written down, and he decided to record them. The book was originally intended for children, but he kept writing until there were four big volumes for adults. The books helped many people understand Lincoln as a real person. Later, Sandburg did write a book for children, *Abe Lincoln Grows Up*. He also wrote a collection of folk songs, *The American Songbag*, including ones he sang as a hobo, such as "I Ride an Old Paint," "The John B. Sails," and "Blow the Man Down." As if this were not enough, Sandburg also reviewed movies for the *Chicago Daily News*, and he even became friends with Charlie Chaplin and other stars.

When Sandburg met the pretty and energetic schoolteacher Lilian Steichen, he knew he had found someone who understood him, believed in his talent, and shared his interests. He was thirty years old when they married. Lilian's parents had been immigrants, too, and she convinced him to return to using the name Carl because it seemed more like him. Lilian's family called her "Paus'l," a word used in Belgium to mean someone dear. But Lilian's sister couldn't say Paus'l and called her Paula instead. Sandburg thought that Paula suited her best.

Carl and Paula Sandburg's lives were never free of struggles. They had very little money. Margaret, their first child, had epilepsy, a condition about which little was known and for which there was no medication. In order to earn extra money for medical bills, Sandburg lectured, read poetry, and sang folk songs all over the United States, in addition to his job as a newspaper journalist. Their second child died at birth. Their two youngest, Janet and Helga, were both physically healthy; however, Janet was slow in school, and was hit by a car when she was sixteen, which made her learning problems worse. Neither Margaret nor Janet ever moved away from home.

Sandburg kept writing poetry despite his many hardships. He worked long into the night while Paula cared for the girls. He wrote about people he met and faces he remembered, like the plowboy with a team of horses who made a picture in his mind (see page 18). He wrote about Margaret's blue eyes and little wild wishes (see page 14), the sea pounding the shore (see page 9), and summer grass (see page 22). Sometimes people criticized Sandburg for using free verse, saying it didn't make sense. But Sandburg's work was carefully written and it appealed to ordinary people.

Sandburg was a wonderful storyteller, often telling tales to his daughters. He thought American children needed their own fairy tales, not ones about knights and princesses locked up in castles. He made up stories about simple things that happened in ordinary places to ordinary people like the White Horse Girl and the Blue Wind Boy. He called his *Rootabaga Stories* "nonsense stories with a lot of American fooling in them." Many of his poems contain lines about "fooling" as well, such as "Arithmetic is where numbers fly like pigeons in and out of your head" (see page 17); in "We Must Be Polite" (see page 27), he offers advice about what to do if you meet a gorilla or if an elephant comes to your door.

When he was in his sixties, Sandburg and his family moved to a new home in the mountains of North Carolina with enough room for his books and papers and for Paula and Helga's herd of dairy goats. Helga, who had recently been divorced, lived with them for several years and helped her father with his writing. Sandburg lived in North Carolina until his death on July 22, 1967.

Sandburg received many awards and prizes for his work as a writer and poet. Once asked whether he wanted to be known as a poet, a biographer, or a historian, Sandburg replied that he didn't think it was important what he was called. When a famous reporter asked him what he thought was the worst word in the English language, Sandburg said it was "exclusive," because when you are exclusive you shut people out of your mind and heart. Maybe that is why Carl Sandburg could never settle on one profession and followed his dream of becoming a poet and a writer. Some like to say that he was the eternal hobo—always exploring and trying new things and places—and was never exclusive.

FOG

The fog comes
on little cat feet.

It sits looking
over harbor and city
on silent haunches
and then moves on.

FROM THE SHORE

A lone gray bird,
Dim-dipping, far-flying,
Alone in the shadows and grandeurs and tumults
Of night and the sea
And the stars and storms.

Out over the darkness it wavers and hovers,
Out into the gloom it swings and batters,
Out into the wind and the rain and the vast,
Out into the pit of a great black world,
Where fogs are at battle, sky-driven, sea-blown,
Love of mist and rapture of flight,
Glories of chance and hazards of death
On its eager and palpitant wings.

Out into the deep of the great dark world,
Beyond the long borders where foam and drift
Of the sundering waves are lost and gone
On the tides that plunger and rear and crumble.

grandeurs—*instances of being magnificent*

tumults—*outbursts, commotions*

rapture—*a feeling of intense emotion*

palpitant—*throbbing, beating*

sundering—*parting, breaking apart*

plunger—*to dive*

YOUNG SEA

The sea is never still.
It pounds on the shore
Restless as a young heart,
Hunting.

The sea speaks
And only the stormy hearts
Know what it says:
It is the face
    of a rough mother speaking.

The sea is young.
One storm cleans all the hoar
And loosens the age of it.
I hear it laughing, reckless.

They love the sea,
Men who ride on it
And know they will die
Under the salt of it.

Let only the young come,
  Says the sea.
Let them kiss my face
  And hear me.
I am the last word
  And I tell
Where storms and stars come from.

hoar—*frost*

LAST ANSWERS

I wrote a poem on the mist
And a woman asked me what I meant by it.
I had thought till then only of the beauty of the mist, how
        pearl and gray of it mix and reel,
And change the drab shanties with lighted lamps at
        evening into points of mystery quivering with color.

  I answered:
The whole world was mist once long ago and some day
        it will all go back to mist,
Our skulls and lungs are more water than bone and tissue
And all poets love dust and mist because all the last
        answers
Go running back to dust and mist.

shanties—*little huts or houses*

A Sphinx

Close-mouthed you sat five thousand years and never let
out a whisper,
Processions came by, marchers, asking questions you
answered with gray eyes never blinking, shut lips
never talking.
Not one croak of anything you know has come from your
cat crouch of ages.
I am one of those who know all you know and I keep my
questions: I know the answers you hold.

LITTLE GIRL,
BE CAREFUL WHAT YOU SAY

Little girl, be careful what you say
when you make talk with words, words—
for words are made of syllables
and syllables, child, are made of air—
and air is so thin—air is the breath of God—
air is finer than fire or mist,
finer than water or moonlight,
finer than spider-webs in the moon,
finer than water-flowers in the morning:
     and words are strong, too,
     stronger than rocks or steel
stronger than potatoes, corn, fish, cattle,
and soft, too, soft as little pigeon-eggs,
soft as the music of hummingbird wings.
     So, little girl, when you speak greetings,
when you tell jokes, make wishes or prayers,
     be careful, be careless, be careful,
     be what you wish to be.

MARGARET

Many birds and the beating of wings
Make a flinging reckless hum
In the early morning at the rocks
Above the blue pool
Where the gray shadows swim lazy.

In your blue eyes, O reckless child,
I saw today many little wild wishes,
Eager as the great morning.

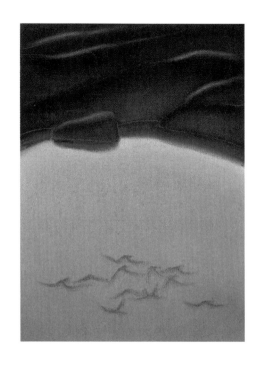

ARITHMETIC

Arithmetic is where numbers fly like pigeons in and out of your head.

Arithmetic tells you how many you lose or win if you know how
      many you had before you lost or won.

Arithmetic is seven eleven all good children go to heaven—or five six
      bundle of sticks.

Arithmetic is numbers you squeeze from your head to your hand to
      your pencil to your paper till you get the answer.

Arithmetic is where the answer is right and everything is nice
      and you can look out of the window and see the blue sky—or the answer is
      wrong and you have to start all over and try again and see how it
      comes out this time.

If you take a number and double it and double it again and then
      double it a few more times, the number gets bigger and bigger and goes
      higher and higher and only arithmetic can tell you what the number is when
      you decide to quit doubling.

Arithmetic is where you have to multiply—and you carry the
      multiplication table in your head and hope you won't lose it.

If you have two animal crackers, one good and one bad, and you
      eat one and a striped zebra with streaks all over him eats the other, how
      many animal crackers will you have if somebody offers you
      five six seven and you say No no no and you say Nay nay nay and you say
      Nix nix nix?

If you ask your mother for one fried egg for breakfast and she
      gives you two fried eggs and you eat both of them, who is better in
      arithmetic, you or your mother?

PLOWBOY

After the last red sunset glimmer,
Black on the line of a low hill rise,
Formed into moving shadows, I saw
A plowboy and two horses lined against the
  gray,
Plowing in the dusk the last furrow.
The turf had a gleam of brown,
And smell of soil was in the air,
And, cool and moist, a haze of April.

I shall remember you long,
Plowboy and horses against the sky in shadow.
I shall remember you and the picture
You made for me,
Turning the turf in the dusk
And haze of an April gloaming.

gloaming—*twilight*

MONOTONE

The monotone of the rain is beautiful,
And the sudden rise and slow relapse
Of the long multitudinous rain.

The sun on the hills is beautiful,
Or a captured sunset sea-flung,
Bannered with fire and gold.

A face I know is beautiful—
With fire and gold of sky and sea,
And the peace of long warm rain.

monotone—*a single, unchanging sound*
multitudinous—*consisting of a crowd or large
number of individuals*

PHIZZOG

This face you got,
This here phizzog you carry around,
You never picked it out for yourself
     at all, at all—did you?
This here phizzog—somebody handed it
     to you—am I right?
Somebody said, "Here's yours, now go see
     what you can do with it."
Somebody slipped it to you and it was like
     a package marked:
"No goods exchanged after being taken away"—
This face you got.

MASK

Fling your red scarf faster and faster, dancer.
It is summer and the sun loves a million green leaves,
     masses of green.
Your red scarf flashes across them calling and a-calling.
The silk and flare of it is a great soprano leading a chorus
Carried along in a rouse of voices reaching for the heart
     of the world.
Your toes are singing to meet the song of your arms:

Let the red scarf go swifter.
Summer and the sun command you.

rouse—*an excited state of being*

Summer Grass

Summer grass aches and whispers.

It wants something; it calls and sings; it pours
 out wishes to the overhead stars.
The rain hears; the rain answers; the rain is slow
 coming; the rain wets the face of the grass.

Summer Stars

Bend low again, night of summer stars.
So near you are, sky of summer stars,
So near, a long-arm man can pick off stars,
Pick off what he wants in the sky bowl,
So near you are, summer stars,
So near, strumming, strumming,
 So lazy and hum-strumming.

SKY TALK

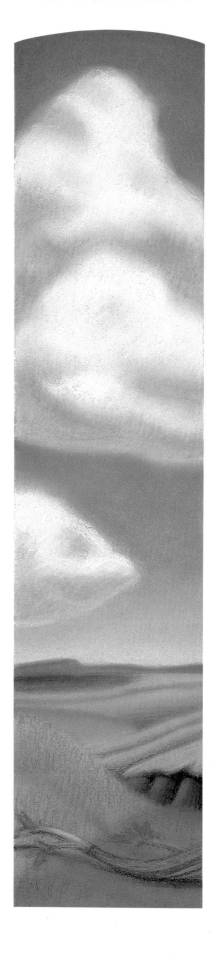

Wool white horses and their heads sag and roll,
Snow white sheep and their tails drag far,
Impossible animals ever more impossible—
      They walk on the sky to say How do you do?
         Or Good-by or Back-soon-maybe.

Or would you say any white flowers come
         more lovely than certain white clouds?
Or would you say any tall mountains beckon,
rise and beckon beyond certain tall walking clouds?

Is there any roll of white sea-horses equal to
         the sky-horse white of certain clouds rolling?

Now we may summon buyers and sellers
and tell them to go buy certain clouds today,
         go sell other clouds tomorrow,
         and we may hear them report
Ups and downs, brisk buying, brisk selling,
      Market unsteady, never so many fluctuations.

Can there be any veering white fluctuations,
      any moving incalculable fluctuations
      quite so incalculable as certain clouds?

fluctuations—*changes of rising and falling*
incalculable—*not capable of being measured or calculated*

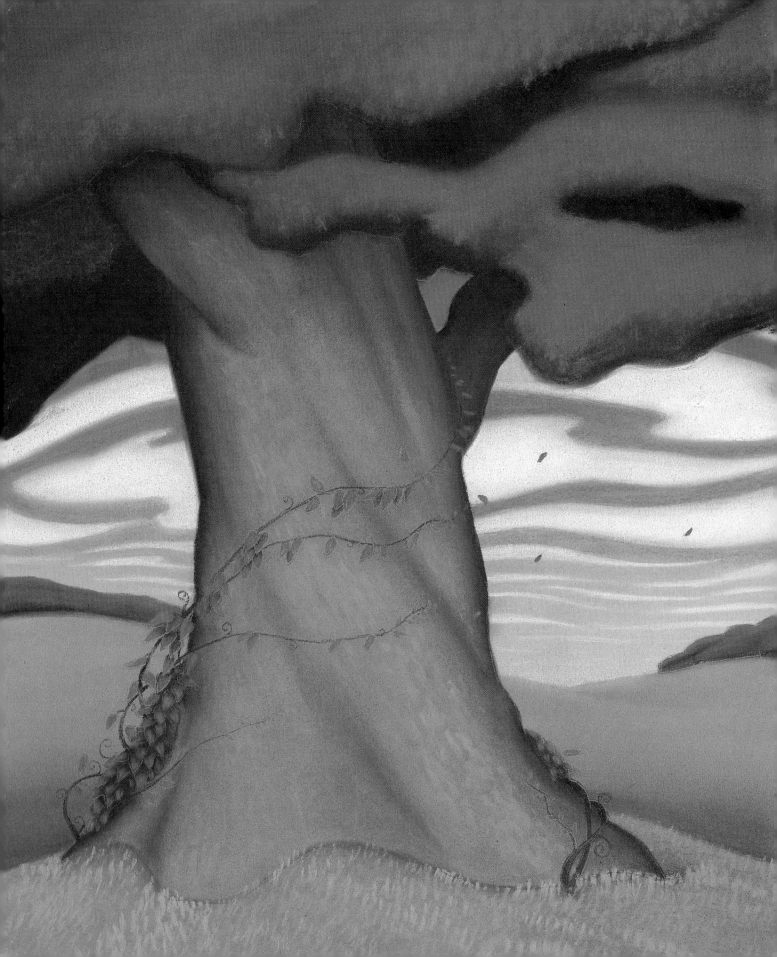

OCTOBER PAINT

Flame blue wisps in the west,
Wrap yourselves in these leaves
And speak to winter about us.
Tell winter the whole story.

Red leaves up the oaken slabs,
You came little and green spats
Four months ago; your climbers
Put scroll after scroll around
The oaken slabs. "Red, come red,"
Some one with an October paint
Pot said. And here you are,
Fifty red arrowheads of leaf paint
Or fifty mystic fox footprints
Or fifty pointed thumbprints.
Hold on, the winds are to come
Blowing, blowing, the gray slabs
Will lose you, the winds will
Flick you away in a whiff
One by one, two by two... Yet
I have heard a rumor whispered;
Tattlers tell it to each other
Like a secret everybody knows...
Next year you will come again.
Up the oaken slabs you will put
Your pointed fox footprints
Green in the early summer
And you will be red arrowheads
In the falltime... Tattlers
Slip this into each other's ears
Like a secret everybody knows.
...If I see some one with an
October paint pot I shall be
Full of respect and say,
"I saw your thumbprints everywhere,
How do you do it?"

THEME IN YELLOW

I spot the hills
With yellow balls in autumn.
I light the prairie cornfields
Orange and tawny gold clusters
And I am called pumpkins.
On the last of October
When dusk is fallen
Children join hands
And circle round me
Singing ghost songs
And love to the harvest moon;
I am a jack-o'-lantern
With terrible teeth
And the children know
I am fooling.

We Must Be Polite

(Lessons for children on how to behave under peculiar circumstances)

1

If we meet a gorilla
what shall we do?
Two things we may do
if we so wish to do.

Speak to the gorilla
very, very respectfully,
"How do you do, sir?"

Or, speak to him with less
distinction of manner,
"Hey, why don't you go back
where you came from?"

2

If an elephant knocks on your door
and asks for something to eat,
there are two things to say:

Tell him there are nothing but cold
victuals in the house and he will do
better next door.

Or say: We have nothing but six bushels
of potatoes—will that be enough for
your breakfast, sir?

victuals (pronouced VITT-els)—
supplies of food

33

RAT RIDDLES

There was a gray rat looked at me
with green eyes out of a rathole.

"Hello, rat," I said,
"Is there any chance for me
to get on to the language of the rats?"

And the green eyes blinked at me,
blinked from a gray rat's rathole.

"Come again," I said,
"Slip me a couple of riddles;
there must be riddles among the rats."

And the green eyes blinked at me
and a whisper came from the gray rathole:
"Who do you think you are and why is a rat?
Where did you sleep last night and why do you sneeze
on Tuesdays? And why is the grave of a rat no
deeper than the grave of a man?"

And the tail of a green-eyed rat
Whipped and was gone at a gray rathole.

A HOMELY WINTER IDYL

Great, long, lean clouds in sullen host
   Along the skyline passed today;
While overhead I've only seen
   A leaden sky the whole day long.

My heart would gloomily have mused
   Had I not seen those queer, old crows
Stop short in their mad frolicking
   And pose for me in long, black rows.

idyl—*a poem that describes something or tells a story*
mused—*thought about or reflected on something*

LANDSCAPE

See the trees lean to the wind's way of learning.
See the dirt of the hills shape to the water's
    way of learning.
See the lift of it all go the way the biggest
    wind and the strongest water want it.

BOXES AND BAGS

The bigger the box the more it holds.

Empty boxes hold the same as empty heads.

Enough small empty boxes thrown into a big empty box fill it full.

A half-empty box says, "Put more in."

A big enough box could hold the world.

Elephants need big boxes to hold a dozen elephant handkerchiefs.

Fleas fold little handkerchiefs and fix them nice and neat in
      flea handkerchief boxes.

Bags lean against each other and boxes stand independent.

Boxes are square with corners unless round with circles.

Box can be piled on box till the whole works comes tumbling.

Pile box on box and the bottom box says, "If you will kindly take
      notice you will see it all rests on me."

Pile box on box and the top one says, "Who falls farthest if or
      when we fall? I ask you."

Box people go looking for boxes and bag people go looking for bags.

SKYSCRAPER

By day the skyscraper looms in the smoke and sun and
      has a soul.
Prairie and valley, streets of the city, pour people into it
      and they mingle among its twenty floors and are
      poured out again back to the streets, prairies and
      valleys.
It is the men and women, boys and girls so poured in and
      out all day that give the building a soul of dreams
      and thoughts and memories.
(Dumped in the sea or fixed in a desert, who would care
      for the building or speak its name or ask a policeman
      the way to it?)

Elevators slide on their cables and tubes catch letters and
      parcels and iron pipes carry gas and water in and
      sewage out.
Wires climb with secrets, carry light and carry words,
      and tell terrors and profits and loves—curses of men
      grappling plans of business and questions of women
      in plots of love.
Hour by hour the caissons reach down to the rock of the
      earth and hold the building to a turning planet.
Hour by hour the girders play as ribs and reach out and
      hold together the stone walls and floors.
Hour by hour the hand of the mason and the stuff of the
      mortar clinch the pieces and parts to the shape an
      architect voted.
Hour by hour the sun and the rain, the air and the rust,
      and the press of time running into centuries, play on
      the building inside and out and use it.

Men who sunk the pilings and mixed the mortar are laid
      in graves where the wind whistles a wild song without
      words.
And so are men who strung the wires and fixed the pipes
      and tubes and those who saw it rise floor by floor.

Souls of them all are here, even the hod carrier begging
      at back doors hundreds of miles away and the brick-layer
      who went to state prison for shooting another
      man while drunk.
(One man fell from a girder and broke his neck at the end
      of a straight plunge—he is here—his soul has gone
      into the stones of the building.)
On the office doors from tier to tier—hundreds of names
      and each name standing for a face written across with
      a dead child, a passionate lover, a driving ambition
      for a million-dollar business or a lobster's ease of life.

Behind the signs on the doors they work and the walls tell
      nothing from room to room.
Ten-dollar-a-week stenographers take letters from corporation
      officers, lawyers, efficiency engineers, and tons of
      letters go bundled from the building to all
      ends of the earth.
Smiles and tears of each office girl go into the soul of the
      building just the same as the master-men who rule
      the building.

Hands of clocks turn to noon hours and each floor empties
      its men and women who go away and eat and come
      back to work.
Toward the end of the afternoon all work slackens and all
      jobs go slower as the people feel day closing on them.

One by one the floors are emptied.... The uniformed
      elevator men are gone. Pails clang...Scrubbers
      work, talking in foreign tongues. Broom and water
      and mop clean from the floors human dust and spit,
      and machine grime of the day.
Spelled in electric fire on the roof are words telling miles
      of houses and people where to buy a thing for
      money. The sign speaks till midnight.

Darkness on the hallways. Voices echo. Silence holds.
   . . . Watchmen walk slow from floor to floor and try
   the doors. Revolvers bulge from their hip pockets.
   . . . Steel safes stand in corners. Money is stacked in them.
A young watchman leans at a window and sees the lights of barges
   butting their way across a harbor, nets of red and white
   lanterns in a railroad yard, and a span of glooms
   splashed with lines of white and blurs of crosses
   and clusters over the sleeping city.
By night the skyscraper looms in the smoke and the stars
   and has a soul.

grappling—*struggling with*
caissons—*box-like structures used in constructing underwater or in*
   working below the earth near a large body of water
stenographers—*office workers employed to take notes*

UNDER A TELEPHONE POLE

I am a copper wire slung in the air,
Slim against the sun I make not even a clear line of
     shadow.
Night and day I keep singing—humming and thrumming:
It is love and war and money; it is the fighting and the
     tears, the work and the want,
Death and laughter of men and women passing through me,
     carrier of your speech,
In the rain and the wet dripping, in the dawn and the
     shine drying,
               A copper wire.

OLD WOMAN

The owl-car clatters along, dogged by the echo
From building and battered paving-stone;
The headlight scoffs at the mist
And fixes its yellow rays in the cold slow rain;
Against a pane I press my forehead
And drowsily look on the walls and sidewalks.

The headlight finds the way
And life is gone from the wet and the welter—
Only an old woman, bloated, disheveled and bleared.
Far-wandering waif of other days,
Huddles for sleep in a doorway,
Homeless.

welter—*rolling or tossing, turmoil*
disheveled—*having mussed up clothing*
bleared—*dimmed, blurred*
waif—*orphan*

DOORS

An open door says, "Come in."
A shut door says, "Who are you?"
Shadows and ghosts go through shut doors.
If a door is shut and you want it shut,
   why open it?
If a door is open and you want it open,
   why shut it?
Doors forget but only doors know what it is
   doors forget.

A Coin

Your western heads here cast on money,
You are the two that fade away together,
  Partners in the mist.

  Lunging buffalo shoulder,
  Lean Indian face,
We who come after where you are gone
Salute your forms on the new nickel.

  You are
  To us:
  The past.

  Runners
  On the prairie:
  Good-by.

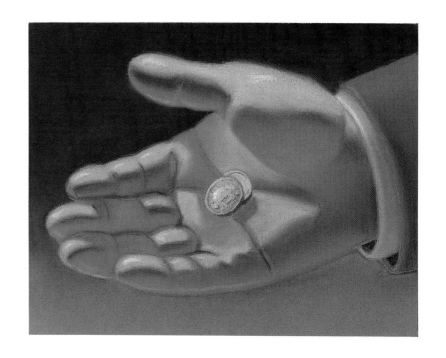

Buffalo Dusk

The buffaloes are gone.
And those who saw the buffaloes are gone.
Those who saw the buffaloes by thousands and how they
   pawed the prairie sod into dust with their hoofs,
   their great heads down pawing on in a great pageant
   of dusk,
Those who saw the buffaloes are gone.
And the buffaloes are gone.

sod—*earth, dirt*
pageant—*elaborate display*

I Sang

I sang to you and the moon
But only the moon remembers.
   I sang
O reckless free-hearted
                    free-throated rhythms,
Even the moon remembers them
And is kind to me.

Jazz Fantasia

Drum on your drums, batter on your banjoes,
sob on the long cool winding saxophones.
Go to it, O jazzmen.

Sling your knuckles on the bottoms of the happy
tin pans, let your trombones ooze, and go husha-
husha-hush with the slippery sand-paper.

Moan like an autumn wind high in the lonesome tree-
tops, moan soft like you wanted somebody terrible,
cry like a racing car slipping away from a motorcycle
cop, bang-bang! you jazzmen, bang altogether drums,
traps, banjoes, horns, tin cans—make two people fight
on the top of a stairway and scratch each other's eyes
in a clinch tumbling down the stairs.

Can the rough stuff…now a Mississippi steamboat
pushes up the night river with a hoo-hoo-hoo-oo…
and the green lanterns calling to the high soft stars
…a red moon rides on the humps of the low river
hills…go to it, O jazzmen.

clinch—*embrace, close hold*

WINDOW

Night from a railroad car window
Is a great, dark, soft thing
Broken across with slashes of light.

SHEEP

Thousands of sheep, soft-footed, black-nosed sheep—one by one going up the hill and over the fence—one by one four-footed pattering up and over—one by one wiggling their stub tails as they take the short jump and go over—one by one silently unless for the multitudinous drumming of their hoofs as they move on and go over—thousands and thousands of them in the gray haze of evening just after sundown—one by one slanting in a long line to pass over the hill—

I am the slow, long-legged Sleepyman and I love you sheep in Persia, California, Argentina, Australia, or Spain—you are the thoughts that help me when I, the Sleepyman, lay my hands on the eyelids of the children of the world at eight o'clock every night—you thousands and thousands of sheep in a procession of dusk making an endless multitudinous drumming on the hills with your hoofs.

BETWEEN TWO HILLS

Between two hills
The old town stands.
The houses loom
And the roofs and trees
And the dusk and the dark,
The damp and the dew
  Are there.

The prayers are said
And the people rest
For sleep is there
And the touch of dreams
  Is over all.

Robert Frost

Edited by Gary D. Schmidt
Illustrated by Henri Sorensen

Robert Frost: A New England Life

IF YOU WALK DOWN A ROAD IN VERMONT IN MID-WINTER, UNDER A bright blue sky with the air so cold it seems to thaw only as you breathe it in, you see mountains piled up against each other, stone fences stretching across fields of dried cornstalks, and white birches with crackling black branches. Your feet crunch against the dry snow, while a crow caws, caws, caws about the cold.

This is the world of Robert Frost's poetry—snow and crows and birches, as well as brooks and asters and hayfields and autumn leaves. Seldom has a poet been so identified with a region as Robert Frost has with New England, though he himself would not have claimed this. His poems have the feel of sudden lines that surprised him. You catch a poem just as it comes, he once said. What he caught were poems about New England—and about life.

On March 26, 1874, Frost was born in San Francisco, which is about as far as you can get from New England and still be in the continental United States. Frost's father was a journalist who edited a city newspaper, and his mother was a teacher. Frost eventually tried his hand at both professions.

His father was born in the South but moved to New Hampshire to become a journalist. He left the region during the Civil War (perhaps because he did not want to be seen as a Yankee) and moved to California. As if to tweak the nose of New England, he named his son after the South's most famous general, Robert E. Lee. But after his father's death in 1885, eleven-year-old Robert, his sister Jeanie, and their mother returned to New England. The family had no money, so they lived with Robert's grandfather in Lawrence, Massachussetts.

It is never easy to return home, though. Frost hated his work as a bobbin boy in his grandfather's mills. He disliked his grandfather's strictness and the way he made Frost's mother feel responsible for his father's death. Soon his mother could stand it no longer. She went a few miles south to Salem, New Hampshire, to teach, settling herself and her family with a nearby farmwife. The pay was poor, so Frost took a job as a cobbler, nailing heels to boots, to help pay the rent.

Frost did well at the village school in Salem. During the next three years, Frost's grandfather offered to pay for the train fare that would allow him to attend Lawrence High School. Frost was elated and soon became the top student in his class.

When Frost was sixteen, he began to write poetry, jotting down words that seemed to just come into his mind. But he was not yet thinking of becoming a poet. Perhaps he was thinking more about Elinor White, with whom he had shared the highest honors in his school when they graduated in 1892.

The years after his graduation were frustrating for Frost. His grandfather demanded that he go on to Dartmouth, but Frost wasn't interested in college. He was interested in poetry, however, and soon all he was doing was wandering through the woods reading a collection of British poems, so he left Dartmouth and returned to Lawrence. He worked in the mills again and kept reading and writing. When he was nineteen, he sent his first poem to a magazine called *The Independent*. It was accepted, and Robert Frost knew he wanted to be a poet.

Even a poet needs income, so he tried his father's profession—writing for a weekly newspaper called *The Sentinel*. He liked the writing, but hated prying into things he thought were none of his business. He quit after only a few months, then taught school with his mother and sister. In 1895, Elinor White came to teach with them, and soon afterward, in December, she and Frost were married. But Frost did not enjoy teaching young children, and there was little money coming in.

The following year, the Frosts had a son. To earn more money the new father decided that he would be a college teacher, but first he had to finish college himself. With help from his grandfather, he began studies at New England's most prestigious university, Harvard, but the courses bored him. He became sick; but even worse, his son Eliot also grew ill, and then died.

There seemed no reason to stay at Harvard. Frost left without finishing, which meant he could not teach college. Elinor begged Frost's grandfather to help them buy a farm.

Grandfather was reluctant, but willing. If Frost would commit himself to working the farm for ten years, his grandfather would pay for it. Frost agreed, and in 1900, he, Elinor, and their new baby daughter settled into a dairy farm in Derry, New Hampshire. During the day, he did all the chores to keep the farm going; at night, when the house was completely still, he wrote poetry. Those were the years when he wrote such poems as "Mending Wall" and "October."

It was hard for Frost to make a go of his rocky farm, especially since he had three more children over the next five years. Money was scarce, but when the director of the Pinkerton Academy heard Frost read one of his poems, he was impressed. He asked Frost to teach an English class two days each week, and Frost agreed. He needed the money for food.

Frost stayed for the ten years he promised his grandfather, and then sold the farm. He had never liked the busy schedule of a farmer, and he suffered from hay fever, so he couldn't cut his own hay. Although editors rejected his poems over the years because they seemed too modern, Frost knew he had to keep trying. The family had to find a place where they could live on little money and where Frost would be free to write his poetry. Perhaps thinking of the British poets he had read at Dartmouth, Frost decided to go to England.

In the autumn of 1912, Frost and his family settled into a small country farmhouse thatched with thick straw. Ignoring the pile of rejection letters that he had received from editors in the U.S., Frost brought thirty of his poems to a publisher in London. Three days later, he heard that they had been accepted for a book. Within a year, this New England poet's life as a professional began: *A Boy's Will* was published in 1913, followed by *North of Boston* the next year. When the books were reprinted in America, Frost said to Elinor, "My book has gone home; we must go too," and so the Frost family returned to New England in 1914.

Frost came back to a country with arms open wide to receive him. Editors who had earlier rejected his poems were anxious to publish them. But his poetry was still not making much money, and his first two books earned him only two hundred dollars.

As the family settled in, Frost looked about his world for inspiration. He saw birches and fields and mountains, and those are what he wrote about. He walked across upland pastures and wrote "The Vantage Point." He explored a forest whose leaves had turned golden in the autumn chill and wrote "The Road Not Taken." He watched cows munching on apples and wrote "The Cow in Apple Time." He saw boys climbing birch trees and wrote "Birches."

The years after his return from England were busy. His poems were praised by critics, and people came to New England to meet him. They also asked him to read at colleges such as Amherst, Harvard, Yale, Dartmouth, and Michigan. The trips interrupted his writing, and he always seemed to come back with a cold, but he went, because the reading brought in money.

As he became better known, Frost was asked to teach—first at Amherst, then at other universities—and his dream of becoming a college teacher finally came true. In fact, in 1920 he even helped to start a college—the Bread Loaf School of English in Vermont. He was a challenging, witty, and sometimes grouchy teacher, once throwing away a whole pile of compositions his students had written. But his students loved him, for he made them think.

In 1923 Frost published *New Hampshire*, which won the Pulitzer Prize, one of the country's most prestigious awards. Seven years later, he won his second Pulitzer for his *Collected Poems*, and then, astonishingly, a third Pulitzer in 1936 for *A Further Range*. No one was surprised when he won his fourth Pulitzer Prize in 1942. These books, together with his teaching and many speaking tours, finally earned him the money that had previously eluded him.

In 1957, Frost attended a dinner in England held in his honor. T.S. Eliot, the greatest English poet then living, gave the toast. He also had lived in New England, and he knew what Frost was writing about. Frost, he said, was writing about the whole world, about feelings and ideas that everyone, everywhere, understood. Those who were there saw that Frost nearly began to weep.

The next year, Frost spoke at Bread Loaf, thinking of that toast by T.S. Eliot. "There ought to be in everything you write some sign that you come from almost anywhere," he said. Perhaps that is what keeps Robert Frost so alive today, even to people who have never set foot in Vermont. In writing about New England, Frost was also writing about everywhere.

Frost became the country's most beloved poet. He received the formal congratulations of the United States Senate when he turned seventy-five, and again a decade later. The next year, he read his poem "The Gift Outright" at the inauguration of President John F. Kennedy. When he died three years later, people around the world mourned, many remembering him for what he was—a great poet.

Poems of
Summer

THE PASTURE

I'm going out to clean the pasture spring;
I'll only stop to rake the leaves away
(And wait to watch the water clear, I may)
I sha'n't be gone long.—You come too.

I'm going out to fetch the little calf
That's standing by the mother. It's so young
It totters when she licks it with her tongue.
I sha'n't be gone long.—You come too.

Robert Frost used "The Pasture" to introduce his poetry. In this poem, he seems to be talking perhaps to a friend, someone he loves, or a stranger who has stopped by. He asks the listener to come out to the pasture with him, to see the things that he will see. But Frost is also asking his reader to come into his world—a world of pastures, leaves, springs, and young calves newly born.

ROSE POGONIAS

A saturated meadow,
　Sun-shaped and jewel-small,
A circle scarcely wider
　Than the trees around were tall;
Where winds were quite excluded,
　And the air was stifling sweet
With the breath of many flowers,—
　A temple of the heat.

There we bowed us in the burning,
　As the sun's right worship is,
To pick where none could miss them
　A thousand orchises;
For though the grass was scattered,
　Yet every second spear
Seemed tipped with wings of color,
　That tinged the atmosphere.

We raised a simple prayer
　Before we left the spot,
That in the general mowing
　That place might be forgot;
Or if not all so favored,
　Obtain such grace of hours,
That none should mow the grass there
　While so confused with flowers.

*Flowers last only a short time, especially
if they are growing in a hayfield, where they
will be cut and harvested along with the hay.
But Frost, thinking about how short and
sweet beauty is, tries in this poem to find a
way to keep the flowers—and their beauty—
from being cut.*

THE TUFT OF FLOWERS

I went to turn the grass once after one
Who mowed it in the dew before the sun.

The dew was gone that made his blade so keen
Before I came to view the leveled scene.

I looked for him behind an isle of trees;
I listened for his whetstone on the breeze.

But he had gone his way, the grass all mown,
And I must be, as he had been,—alone,

"As all must be," I said within my heart,
"Whether they work together or apart."

But as I said it, swift there passed me by
On noiseless wing a bewildered butterfly,

Seeking with memories grown dim o'er night
Some resting flower of yesterday's delight.

And once I marked his flight go round and round,
As where some flower lay withering on the ground.

And then he flew as far as eye could see,
And then on tremulous wing came back to me.

I thought of questions that have no reply,
And would have turned to toss the grass to dry;

But he turned first, and led my eye to look
At a tall tuft of flowers beside a brook,

A leaping tongue of bloom the scythe had spared
Beside a reedy brook the scythe had bared.

The mower in the dew had loved them thus,
By leaving them to flourish, not for us,

Nor yet to draw one thought of ours to him,
But from sheer morning gladness at the brim.

The butterfly and I had lit upon,
Nevertheless, a message from the dawn,

That made me hear the wakening birds around,
And hear his long scythe whispering to the ground,

And feel a spirit kindred to my own;
So that henceforth I worked no more alone;

But glad with him, I worked as with his aid,
And weary, sought at noon with him the shade;

And dreaming, as it were, held brotherly speech
With one whose thought I had not hoped to reach.

"Men work together," I told him from the heart,
"Whether they work together or apart."

After a hayfield has been mown, the long grass has to be turned over after a time so that it will dry on both sides and not rot. This can be a boring job, especially if you are doing it alone and by hand. That's how this poem begins—with a man working alone and facing a dull day—but not how it ends. Written in couplets (pairs of rhyming lines), the poem seems to mirror the rhythm of a scythe.

AN ENCOUNTER

Once on the kind of day called "weather breeder,"
When the heat slowly hazes and the sun
By its own power seems to be undone,
I was half boring through, half climbing through
A swamp of cedar. Choked with oil of cedar
And scurf of plants, and weary and over-heated,
And sorry I ever left the road I knew,
I paused and rested on a sort of hook
That had me by the coat as good as seated,
And since there was no other way to look,
Looked up toward heaven, and there against the blue,
Stood over me a resurrected tree,
A tree that had been down and raised again—
A barkless specter. He had halted too,
As if for fear of treading upon me.
I saw the strange position of his hands—
Up at his shoulders, dragging yellow strands
Of wire with something in it from men to men.
"You here?" I said. "Where aren't you nowadays?
And what's the news you carry—if you know?
And tell me where you're off for—Montreal?
Me? I'm not off for anywhere at all.
Sometimes I wander out of beaten ways
Half looking for the orchid Calypso."

At times in his poetry, Frost brings together two images that
you would never expect to see together. In this poem, he is
out for a walk in the woods and comes upon "a barkless
specter." Watch for the clues that Frost gives as to what this
specter might be, and why it is so unusual to come upon it in
the middle of the woods.

GHOST HOUSE

I dwell in a lonely house I know
That vanished many a summer ago,
  And left no trace but the cellar walls,
  And a cellar in which the daylight falls,
And the purple-stemmed wild raspberries grow.

O'er ruined fences the grapevines shield
The woods come back to the mowing field;
  The orchard tree has grown one copse
  Of new wood and old where the woodpecker
    chops;
The footpath down to the well is healed.

I dwell with a strangely aching heart
In that vanished abode there far apart
  On that disused and forgotten road
  That has no dust-bath now for the toad.
Night comes; the black bats tumble and dart;

The whippoorwill is coming to shout
And hush and cluck and flutter about:
  I hear him begin far enough away
  Full many a time to say his say
Before he arrives to say it out.

It is under the small, dim, summer star.
I know not who these mute folks are
  Who share the unlit place with me—
  Those stones out under the low-limbed tree
Doubtless bear names that the mosses mar.

They are tireless folk, but slow and sad,
Though two, close-keeping, are lass and lad,—
  With none among them that ever sings,
  And yet, in view of how many things,
As sweet companions as might be had.

The house in this poem has been long abandoned; nothing is left of it but the cellar walls. It was probably once a farmhouse, since the raspberries, grapevines, and mowing field all suggest that the land around it was once farmed. As a child plays in the forgotten rooms, he imagines those who once lived there.

A GIRL'S GARDEN

A neighbor of mine in the village
  Likes to tell how one spring
When she was a girl on the farm, she did
  A childlike thing.

One day she asked her father
  To give her a garden plot
To plant and tend and reap herself,
  And he said, "Why not?"

In casting about for a corner
  He thought of an idle bit
Of walled-off ground where a shop had stood,
  And he said, "Just it."

And he said, "That ought to make you
  An ideal one-girl farm,
And give you a chance to put some strength
  On your slim-jim arm."

It was not enough of a garden,
  Her father said, to plow;
So she had to work it all by hand,
  But she don't mind now.

She wheeled the dung in the wheelbarrow
  Along a stretch of road;
But she always ran away and left
  Her not-nice load,

And hid from anyone passing.
  And then she begged the seed.
She says she thinks she planted one
  Of all things but weed.

A hill each of potatoes,
  Radishes, lettuce, peas,
Tomatoes, beets, beans, pumpkins, corn
  And even fruit trees.

And yes, she has long mistrusted
  That a cider apple tree
In bearing there today is hers,
  Or at least may be.

Her crop was a miscellany
  When all was said and done,
A little bit of everything,
  A great deal of none.

Now when she sees in the village
  How village things go,
Just when it seems to come in right,
  She says, "*I* know!

"It's as when I was a farmer—"
  Oh, never by way of advice!
And she never sins by telling the tale
  To the same person twice.

This poem about a young girl's garden is meant to be humorous, so Frost gives it a light and bouncing rhythm. But even though the story is a funny one, Frost makes a serious point about human nature.

THE VANTAGE POINT

If tired of trees I seek again mankind,
  Well I know where to hie me—in the dawn,
  To a slope where the cattle keep the lawn.
There amid lolling juniper reclined,
Myself unseen, I see in white defined
  Far off the homes of men, and farther still,
  The graves of men on an opposing hill,
Living or dead, whichever are to mind.

And if by noon I have too much of these,
  I have but to turn on my arm, and lo,
  The sunburned hillside sets my face aglow,
My breathing shakes the bluet like a breeze,
  I smell the earth, I smell the bruisèd plant.
  I look into the crater of the ant.

A vantage point is a place that allows you to see all around you. In this poem Frost looks at two different worlds—nature and humanity—and seems at home in both.

HYLA BROOK

By June our brook's run out of song and speed.
Sought for much after that, it will be found
Either to have gone groping underground
(And taken with it all the Hyla breed
That shouted in the mist a month ago,
Like ghost of sleigh bells in a ghost of snow)—
Or flourished and come up in jewel-weed,
Weak foliage that is blown upon and bent,
Even against the way its waters went.
Its bed is left a faded paper sheet
Of dead leaves stuck together by the heat—
A brook to none but who remember long.
This as it will be seen is other far
Than with brooks taken otherwhere in song.
We love the things we love for what they are.

*Many poems are written to celebrate beautiful
rivers and pleasant streams, but this one is about
a brook that can run dry. Still, for the poet there
seems to be something quite special about it.*

69

Poems of
Autumn

THE LAST WORD
OF A BLUEBIRD

As told to a child

As I went out a Crow
In a low voice said, "Oh,
I was looking for you.
How do you do?
I just came to tell you
To tell Lesley (will you?)
That her little Bluebird
Wanted me to bring word
That the north wind last night
That made the stars bright
And made ice on the trough

Almost made him cough
His tail feathers off.
He just had to fly!
But he sent her Good-by,
And said to be good,
And wear her red hood,
And look for skunk tracks
In the snow with an ax—
And do everything!
And perhaps in the spring
He would come back and sing."

In this poem, a crow speaks, bringing the message of a bluebird who is flying south for the winter.

THE ROAD NOT TAKEN

Two roads diverged in a yellow wood,
And sorry I could not travel both
And be one traveler, long I stood
And looked down one as far as I could
To where it bent in the undergrowth;

Then took the other, as just as fair,
And having perhaps the better claim,
Because it was grassy and wanted wear;
Though as for that the passing there
Had worn them really about the same,

And both that morning equally lay
In leaves no step had trodden black.
Oh, I kept the first for another day!
Yet knowing how way leads on to way,
I doubted if I should ever come back.

I shall be telling this with a sigh
Somewhere ages and ages hence:
Two roads diverged in a wood, and I—
I took the one less traveled by,
And that has made all the difference.

We all know the feel of a cool autumn day, when we can shuffle our feet through fallen leaves and kick up the smells of the season. This is a poem about such a walk, about coming to a fork in the path, and about making choices in our lives.

IN HARDWOOD GROVES

The same leaves over and over again!
They fall from giving shade above
To make one texture of faded brown
And fit the earth like a leather glove.

Before the leaves can mount again
To fill the trees with another shade,
They must go down past things coming up.
They must go down into the dark decayed.

They *must* be pierced by flowers and put
Beneath the feet of dancing flowers.
However it is in some other world
I know that this is the way in ours.

*Walking through a grove of hardwood trees—perhaps maples or oaks—
Frost recognizes that before things are raised up, they must fall down. He uses
some startling images, such as flowers piercing dead leaves, and a simile, in
which he compares the leaves to a leather glove.*

OCTOBER

O hushed October morning mild,
Thy leaves have ripened to the fall;
Tomorrow's wind, if it be wild,
Should waste them all.
The crows above the forest call;
Tomorrow they may form and go.
O hushed October morning mild,
Begin the hours of this day slow.
Make the day seem to us less brief.
Hearts not averse to being beguiled,
Beguile us in the way you know.
Release one leaf at break of day;
At noon release another leaf;
One from our trees, one far away.
Retard the sun with gentle mist;
Enchant the land with amethyst.
Slow, slow!
For the grapes' sake, if they were all,
Whose leaves already are burnt with frost,
Whose clustered fruit must else be lost—
For the grapes' sake along the wall.

A New England October can have days that seem
like winter. In this poem, Frost wants to put off those
wintry days and keep the golden fullness of autumn.
He speaks directly to October, in a kind of prayer.

THE COW IN APPLE TIME

Something inspires the only cow of late
To make no more of a wall than an open gate,
And think no more of wall-builders than fools.
Her face is flecked with pomace and she drools
A cider syrup. Having tasted fruit,
She scorns a pasture withering to the root.
She runs from tree to tree where lie and sweeten
The windfalls spiked with stubble and worm-eaten.
She leaves them bitten when she has to fly.
She bellows on a knoll against the sky.
Her udder shrivels and the milk goes dry.

In this poem a cow has left the dry grass of its pasture and has started to eat fallen apples. Frost uses couplets—pairs of rhyming lines—to give the poem a light and pleasing rhythm. But something happens and Frost points it out by changing from couplets to three lines rhyming together.

A LATE WALK

When I go up through the mowing field,
  The headless aftermath,
Smooth-laid like thatch with the heavy dew,
  Half closes the garden path.

And when I come to the garden ground,
  The whir of sober birds
Up from the tangle of withered weeds
  Is sadder than any words.

A tree beside the wall stands bare,
  But a leaf that lingered brown,
Disturbed, I doubt not, by my thought,
  Comes softly rattling down.

I end not far from my going forth,
  By picking the faded blue
Of the last remaining aster flower
  To carry again to you.

In late autumn, you can sometimes walk through a field and see things that remind you of summer. Here, Frost finds one last flower, an aster, and brings it back as a reminder.

AFTER APPLE-PICKING

My long two-pointed ladder's sticking through a tree
Toward heaven still,
And there's a barrel that I didn't fill
Beside it, and there may be two or three
Apples I didn't pick upon some bough.
But I am done with apple-picking now.
Essence of winter sleep is on the night,
The scent of apples: I am drowsing off.
I cannot rub the strangeness from my sight
I got from looking through a pane of glass
I skimmed this morning from the drinking trough
And held against the world of hoary grass.
It melted, and I let it fall and break.

But I was well
Upon my way to sleep before it fell,
And I could tell
What form my dreaming was about to take.
Magnified apples appear and disappear,
Stem end and blossom end,
And every fleck of russet showing clear.
My instep arch not only keeps the ache,
It keeps the pressure of a ladder-round.
I feel the ladder sway as the boughs bend.
And I keep hearing from the cellar bin
The rumbling sound
Of load on load of apples coming in.
For I have had too much
Of apple-picking: I am overtired
Of the great harvest I myself desired.
There were ten thousand thousand fruit to touch,
Cherish in hand, lift down, and not let fall.
For all
That struck the earth,
No matter if not bruised or spiked with stubble,
Went surely to the cider-apple heap
As of no worth.
One can see what will trouble
This sleep of mine, whatever sleep it is.
Were he not gone,
The woodchuck could say whether its like his
Long sleep, as I describe its coming on,
Or just some human sleep.

Apple-picking can be slow work. Each apple must be picked by hand, while you hold yourself secure on the ladder with your legs. Any apple that falls or is dropped will bruise and then rot, spoiling any other apples that are stored with it. In this poem, the weather is starting to turn wintry—there is already ice on the water trough—and Frost is looking forward to a long winter's sleep.

GOING FOR WATER

The well was dry beside the door,
  And so we went with pail and can
Across the fields behind the house
  To seek the brook if still it ran;

Not loth to have excuse to go,
  Because the autumn eve was fair
(Though chill), because the fields were ours,
  And by the brook our woods were there.

We ran as if to meet the moon
  That slowly danced behind the trees,
The barren boughs without the leaves,
  Without the birds, without the breeze.

But once within the wood, we paused
  Like gnomes that hid us from the moon,
Ready to run to hiding new,
  With laughter when she found us soon.

Each laid on other a staying hand
  To listen ere we dared to look,
And in the hush we joined to make
  We heard, we knew we heard the brook

A note as from a single place,
  A slender tinkling fall that made
Now drops that floated on the pool
  Like pearls, and now a silver blade.

It is late autumn in this poem, and the brooks are starting to freeze up. But late at night, two people watch the moon rise and go toward the brook, and they know by its sound that the brook is still open.

Out, Out—

The buzz saw snarled and rattled in the yard
And made dust and dropped stove-length sticks of wood,
Sweet-scented stuff when the breeze drew across it.
And from there those that lifted eyes could count
Five mountain ranges one behind the other
Under the sunset far into Vermont.
And the saw snarled and rattled, snarled and rattled,
As it ran light, or had to bear a load.
And nothing happened: day was all but done.
Call it a day, I wish they might have said
To please the boy by giving him the half hour
That a boy counts so much when saved from work.
His sister stood beside them in her apron
To tell them "Supper." At the word, the saw,
As if to prove saws knew what supper meant,
Leaped out at the boy's hand, or seemed to leap—
He must have given the hand. However it was,
Neither refused the meeting. But the hand!
The boy's first outcry was a rueful laugh,
As he swung toward them holding up the hand
Half in appeal, but half as if to keep
The life from spilling. Then the boy saw all—
Since he was old enough to know, big boy
Doing a man's work, though a child at heart—
He saw all spoiled. "Don't let them cut my hand off—
The doctor, when he comes. Don't let him, sister!"
So. But the hand was gone already.
The doctor put him in the dark of ether.
He lay and puffed his lips out with his breath.
And then—the watcher at his pulse took fright.
No one believed. They listened at his heart.
Little—less—nothing!—and that ended it.
No more to build on there. And they, since they
Were not the one dead, turned to their affairs.

This is a story about a boy cutting wood to use for winter fires. The scene starts calm and peaceful, but there is a dreadful accident. The last line of the poem is painful. Is the speaker saying that these people were heartless? Or is he saying that life must always go on, even in the face of death?

Poems of
Winter

Now Close the Windows

Now close the windows and hush all the fields:
  If the trees must, let them silently toss;
No bird is singing now, and if there is,
  Be it my loss.

It will be long ere the marshes resume,
  It will be long ere the earliest bird:
So close the windows and not hear the wind,
  But see all wind-stirred.

When winter comes in New England, houses need to be shut against the cold. This is a poem about closing the windows, but it is also about being comfortable at home, looking out from a warm room to the cold outside.

WIND AND
WINDOW FLOWER

Lovers, forget your love,
  And list to the love of these.
She a window flower,
  And he a winter breeze.

When the frosty window veil
  Was melted down at noon,
And the caged yellow bird
  Hung over her in tune,

He marked her through the pane
  He could not help but mark,
And only passed her by,
  To come again at dark.

He was a winter wind,
  Concerned with ice and snow,
Dead weeds and unmated birds,
  And little of love could know.

But he sighed upon the sill,
  He gave the sash a shake,
As witness all within
  Who lay that night awake.

Perchance he half prevailed
  To win her for the flight
From the firelit looking-glass
  And warm stove-window light.

But the flower leaned aside
  And thought of naught to say,
And morning found the breeze
  A hundred miles away.

It is hard to imagine a winter wind loving a window flower, especially when the flower is set against the window as a reminder that spring will come. Perhaps this is what the wind comes to realize as well, because the flower is not interested in him.

85

A PATCH OF OLD SNOW

There's a patch of old snow in a corner
  That I should have guessed
Was a blow-away paper the rain
  Had brought to rest.

It is speckled with grime as if
  Small print overspread it,
The news of a day I've forgotten—
  If I ever read it.

Toward the end of winter, when most of the snow has melted, Frost finds a small patch of dirty snow, perhaps shaded from the sun. Watch how this single image makes him think about the past.

GOOD HOURS

I had for my winter evening walk—
No one at all with whom to talk,
But I had the cottages in a row
Up to their shining eyes in snow.

And I thought I had the folk within:
I had the sound of a violin;
I had a glimpse through curtain laces
Of youthful forms and youthful faces.

I had such company outward bound.
I went till there were no cottages found.
I turned and repented, but coming back
I saw no window but that was black.

Over the snow my creaking feet
Disturbed the slumbering village street
Like profanation, by your leave,
At ten o'clock of a winter eve.

In many of Frost's poems he walks along a path and comments on what he sees. Here, on a cold winter's night, he feels the companionship of those inside the houses he passes.

THE WOOD-PILE

Out walking in the frozen swamp one gray day,
I paused and said, "I will turn back from here.
No, I will go on farther—and we shall see."
The hard snow held me, save where now and then
One foot went through. The view was all in lines
Straight up and down of tall slim trees
Too much alike to mark or name a place by
So as to say for certain I was here
Or somewhere else: I was just far from home.
A small bird flew before me. He was careful
To put a tree between us when he lighted,
And say no word to tell me who he was
Who was so foolish as to think what *he* thought.
He thought that I was after him for a feather—
The white one in his tail; like one who takes
Everything said as personal to himself.
One flight out sideways would have undeceived him.
And then there was a pile of wood for which
I forgot him and let his little fear
Carry him off the way I might have gone,
WIthout so much as wishing him good-night.
He went behind it to make his last stand.
It was a cord of maple, cut and split
And piled—and measured, four by four by eight.
And not another like it could I see.
No runner tracks in this year's snow looped near it.

And it was older sure than this year's cutting,
Or even last year's or the year's before.
The wood was gray and the bark warping off it
And the pile somewhat sunken. Clematis
Had wound strings round and round it like a bundle.
What held it though on one side was a tree
Still growing, and on one a stake and prop,
These latter about to fall. I thought that only
Someone who lived in turning to fresh tasks
Could so forget his handiwork on which
He spent himself, the labor of his ax,
And leave it there far from a useful fireplace
To warm the frozen swamp as best it could
With the slow smokeless burning of decay.

In New England, wood for winter is cut the previous winter so that it can be slid on snow out of the woods. Here, a neatly stacked wood-pile seems ready to be taken out, but it has stood there for some time, rotting in the snow. The image makes Frost think about what might have happened.

STORM FEAR

When the wind works against us in the dark,
And pelts with snow
The lower chamber window on the east,
And whispers with a sort of stifled bark,
The beast,
"Come out! Come out!"—
It costs no inward struggle not to go,
Ah, no!

I count our strength,
Two and a child,
Those of us not asleep subdued to mark
How the cold creeps as the fire dies at length—
How drifts are piled,
Dooryard and road ungraded,
Till even the comforting barn grows far away,
And my heart owns a doubt
Whether 'tis in us to arise with day
And save ourselves unaided.

As in "Now Close the Windows" (page 32), Frost thinks about his family watching the winter from their warm house, but this time there is a fearful snowstorm.

Poems of
Spring

A PRAYER IN SPRING

Oh, give us pleasure in the flowers today;
And give us not to think so far away
As the uncertain harvest; keep us here
All simply in the springing of the year.

Oh, give us pleasure in the orchard white,
Like nothing else by day, like ghosts by night;
And make us happy in the happy bees,
The swarm dilating round the perfect trees.

And make us happy in the darting bird
That suddenly above the bees is heard,
The meteor that thrusts in with needle bill,
And off a blossom in mid air stands still.

For this is love and nothing else is love,
The which it is reserved for God above
To sanctify to what far ends He will,
But which it only needs that we fulfill.

Frost often wrote about time, about how things change and cannot stay the way they are. In this poem he
looks around him and sees the glorious beauty of a spring day, and he prays that it could somehow be kept so
that it would not disappear. In fact, the poet sees the day as being love itself, something that is sanctified; but
even as he utters the prayer, he knows that it cannot be answered.

A TIME TO TALK

When a friend calls to me from the road
And slows his horse to a meaning walk,
I don't stand still and look around
On all the hills I haven't hoed,
And shout from where I am, "What is it?"
No, not as there is a time to talk.
I thrust my hoe in the mellow ground,
Blade-end up and five feet tall,
And plod: I go up to the stone wall
For a friendly visit.

A gardener in the middle of his work may not always want to stop his summertime hoeing, but in this poem the gardener pauses for a friend. He is quite different from the neighbor in "Mending Wall" (page 46), who will not interrupt his work for a friendly chat. The last line is short, as though he is stopping the poem so he can go for his visit.

To the Thawing Wind

Come with rain, O loud Southwester!
Bring the singer, bring the nester;
Give the buried flower a dream;
Make the settled snowbank steam;
Find the brown beneath the white;
But whate'er you do tonight,
Bathe my window, make it flow,
Melt it as the ice will go;
Melt the glass and leave the sticks
Like a hermit's crucifix;
Burst into my narrow stall;
Swing the picture on the wall;
Run the rattling pages o'er;
Scatter poems on the floor;
Turn the poet out of door.

First the poem calls to the thawing wind, asking it to bring an end to winter and to usher in spring. But soon it changes, as we learn that the speaker is also a poet. By the end he is asking the wind to bring him inspiration for his poetry, to bring him and it new life outdoors.

PEA BRUSH

I walked down alone Sunday after church
   To the place where John has been cutting trees,
To see for myself about the birch
   He said I could have to brush my peas.

The sun in the new-cut narrow gap
   Was hot enough for the first of May,
And stifling hot with the odor of sap
   From stumps still bleeding their life away.

The frogs that were peeping a thousand shrill
   Wherever the ground was low and wet,
The minute they heard my step went still
   To watch me and see what I came to get.

Birch boughs enough piled everywhere!—
   All fresh and sound from the recent ax.
Time someone came with cart and pair
   And got them off the wild flowers' backs.

They might be good for garden things
   To curl a little finger round,
The same as you seize cat's-cradle strings
   And lift themselves up off the ground.

Small good to anything growing wild,
   They were crooking many a trillium
That had budded before the boughs were piled
   And since it was coming up had to come.

Birch boughs can be good for staking up peas, because peas send little tendrils like fingers to climb up stakes. But when Frost finds some birch boughs in this poem, they are doing something quite different.

BIRCHES

When I see birches bend to left and right
Across the lines of straighter darker trees,
I like to think some boy's been swinging them.
But swinging doesn't bend them down to stay
As ice storms do. Often you must have seen them
Loaded with ice a sunny winter morning
After a rain. They click upon themselves
As the breeze rises, and turn many-colored
As the stir cracks and crazes their enamel.
Soon the sun's warmth makes them shed crystal shells
Shattering and avalanching on the snow-crust—
Such heaps of broken glass to sweep away
You'd think the inner dome of heaven had fallen.
They are dragged to the withered bracken by the load,
And they seem not to break; though once they are bowed
So low for long, they never right themselves:
You may see their trunks arching in the woods
Years afterwards, trailing their leaves on the ground
Like girls on hands and knees that throw their hair
Before them over their heads to dry in the sun.
But I was going to say when Truth broke in
With all her matter of fact about the ice-storm
I should prefer to have some boy bend them
As he went out and in to fetch the cows—
Some boy too far from town to learn baseball,
Whose only play was what he found himself,
Summer or winter, and could play alone.
One by one he subdued his father's trees
By riding them down over and over again
Until he took the stiffness out of them,
And not one but hung limp, not one was left
For him to conquer. He learned all there was
To learn about not launching out too soon
And so not carrying the tree away
Clear to the ground. He always kept his poise
To the top branches, climbing carefully
With the same pains you use to fill a cup
Up to the brim, and even above the brim.

Then he flung outward, feet first, with a swish,
Kicking his way down through the air to the ground.
So was I once myself a swinger of birches.
And so I dream of going back to be.
It's when I'm weary of considerations,
And life is too much like a pathless wood
Where your face burns and tickles with the cobwebs
Broken across it, and one eye is weeping
From a twig's having lashed across it open.
I'd like to get away from earth awhile
And then come back to it and begin over.
May no fate willfully misunderstand me
And half grant what I wish and snatch me away
Not to return. Earth's the right place for love:
I don't know where it's likely to go better.
I'd like to go by climbing a birch tree,
And climb black branches up a snow-white trunk
Toward heaven, till the tree could bear no more,
But dipped its top and set me down again.
That would be good both going and coming back.
One could do worse than be a swinger of birches.

Birches are flexible trees. You can climb up into one until it can barely support your weight, then kick out, and the tree will bow you to the ground, and then lift you up again. For Frost, that movement suggests a much larger meaning about how we are to live our lives.

MENDING WALL

Something there is that doesn't love a wall,
That sends the frozen-ground swell under it,
And spills the upper boulders in the sun;
And makes gaps even two can pass abreast.
The work of hunters is another thing:
I have come after them and made repair
Where they have left not one stone on a stone,
But they would have the rabbit out of hiding,
To please the yelping dogs. The gaps I mean,
No one has seen them made or heard them made,
But at spring mending-time we find them there.
I let my neighbor know beyond the hill;
And on a day we meet to walk the line
And set the wall between us once again.
We keep the wall between us as we go.
To each the boulders that have fallen to each.
And some are loaves and some so nearly balls
We have to use a spell to make them balance:
"Stay where you are until our backs are turned."
We wear our fingers rough with handling them.
Oh, just another kind of outdoor game,
One on a side. It comes to little more:
There where it is we do not need the wall:
He is all pine and I am apple orchard.
My apple trees will never get across
And eat the cones under his pines, I tell him.
He only says, "Good fences make good neighbors."
Spring is the mischief in me, and I wonder
If I could put a notion in his head:
"*Why* do they make good neighbors? Isn't it
Where there are cows? But here there are no cows.
Before I built a wall I'd ask to know
What I was walling in or walling out,
And to whom I was like to give offense.
Something there is that doesn't love a wall,
That wants it down." I could say "Elves" to him,
But it's not elves exactly, and I'd rather
He said it for himself. I see him there,

Bringing a stone grasped firmly by the top
In each hand, like an old-stone savage armed.
He moves in darkness as it seems to me,
Not of woods only and the shade of trees.
He will not go behind his father's saying,
And he likes having thought of it so well
He says again, "Good fences make good neighbors."

*If you own a rock wall—and there are many of
these in New England, spread across fields to mark
the boundaries of land—each spring you need to
walk along the wall and replace the stones that the
winter ice or rabbit hunters have knocked to the
ground. But this year, while he lugs the stones, Frost
begins to wonder why he needs the fence at all. His
neighbor has a ready answer.*

Emily Dickinson

Edited by Frances Schoonmaker Bolin
Illustrated by Chi Chung

Introduction

"HOPE IS THE THING WITH FEATHERS," WROTE EMILY DICKINSON. SHE wrote about hope, as well as flowers, birds, people, life, and death—ordinary things. But she had such a vivid imagination that she seemed to get inside these things and look at them in a new way.

Because she had imagination, Emily could write about places she had never been and things she had never seen. Once she wrote (see page 43):

> I never saw a moor,
> I never saw the sea,
> Yet know I how the heather looks,
> And what a wave must be.

In her mind, Emily could walk her dog, Carlo, along a little path, and visit—not the neighbors, but the sea. Sailing ships, or frigates, were on the upper floor and mermaids came up from the basement, as if the sea were a big house. The sea acted as if it would eat her up. It filled her shoes and followed her all the way to town (see page 11). In her imagintion, Emily travelled all over the world.

When Emily was a girl, almost everyone in Amherst, Massachusetts, knew the Dickinsons. Her grandfather helped to found Amherst College, and her father, Edward, a lawyer, was the treasurer of the college. Edward was a very proper and religious man. Every morning and evening, he read to the family from the Bible and led them in prayer. Every Sunday the family went to the Congregational church. Edward Dickinson also served as United States congressman from Massachusetts for a short time. He was so well known that people called him "Squire" Dickinson.

Emily's mother, Emily Norcross Dickinson, was known for her fine cooking. Austin, Emily's brother, was three years older and known for being very bright. He became a lawyer and the treasurer of Amherst College, just like his father. Her sister, Lavinia, whom everyone called Vinnie, was known to be outspoken and witty. She was also much prettier than Emily.

In such an important family, Emily may have seemed to some like a real "nobody." But inside she knew she was somebody special. She played with this thought in "I'm nobody! Who are you?" (see page 12) and at another time told her brother that "bigness" does not come from outside a person, but is something inside.

In many ways, Emily was much like other girls. She enjoyed simple pleasures, such as parties and social and church activities. She liked to gather flowers in the hills with friends, and collected and pressed the flowers. (Once she told her brother that she knew where all the best flowers were, as if each had a house number.) She kept the family garden and loved to plant wildflowers along with the garden flowers. With such ordinary ways, no one suspected that one day she would be the most famous person from Amherst.

Emily loved school, but when she was old enough to attend Amherst Academy, she felt too shy to go alone. She begged her parents to let Vinnie go, too, although Vinnie was much younger. Emily argued that she had been teaching Vinnie to read and that Vinnie was better at arithmetic than she was.

Emily never outgrew this shyness. She was shy around strangers, but when she got to know them, she was witty and fun to be with. People who knew her were also able to accept the odd things she sometimes did, such as the time when she hid from a train. Her father had worked to get the railroad to build a track through Amherst, and everyone in town was excited to see the train make its first trip. Emily, however, hid in the woods where she could watch without being seen!

Perhaps Emily got some of her odd and unpredictable ways, as well as her vision of ordinary things as beautiful and wonderful, from her father. Edward once rang the church bells to call everyone in town out to see a spectacular sunset. No one could have imagined the dignified Edward Dickinson doing such a thing.

Emily began to write poetry when she was in her teens. Nobody in her family was especially interested in writing. But Emily wrote anyway, jotting little notes and verses, particularly Valentine messages. At seventeen, Emily went away to Mount Holyoke Seminary for a year. She was very homesick and wrote many letters home. Austin wrote her back and his letters always cheered her.

It was Austin who wrote Emily about Benjamin Newton, a law student studying with her father. When Emily returned home, she and Ben became good friends, discussing books that Ben loaned to her. Emily's father did not approve of Ben's books, for he felt they contained too many new, liberal ideas. So, to avoid arguments, Ben hid the books in the bushes near the front door when he came to call, and later Emily or Austin collected them.

When Ben left Amherst, he and Emily wrote to each other. Ben was one of the few people who showed an interest in Emily's poetry. He wrote in her autograph album, "All can write autographs, but few paragraphs…."

Not many years later, Benjamin died. Emily was so shocked and sad that she could hardly believe it was true. Sometime later, she began to write poems about death, a part of life that Emily wondered and wrote about for the rest of her life. In "I have not told my garden yet" (see page 41), she imagines her own death.

In Emily's time, people thought that marriage offered the best prospects for a woman. Many young men enjoyed Emily's and Vinnie's company, but neither of the sisters ever married. Some people thought that Emily was too free-spirited to marry.

Austin got married and built a house next door. But unmarried young women generally lived at home in those days. Emily continued to tend the garden and became a good cook, like her mother. Her father refused to eat bread baked by anyone else. But Emily hated housecleaning, so Vinnie performed those tasks and left the kitchen to Emily.

In the evenings, Emily practiced the piano or read. Her nose was in a book almost every spare moment. She often said that books were the best company. A book can "take us lands away," she wrote (see page 44).

Emily continued to be very shy. As she grew older, she began to spend less and less time in town, and by the time she was forty, she almost never left home. The only place she went was next door to see Austin and his wife, Sue, always by the little path through the backyard. She hardly saw anyone except her family and some neighborhood children. When friends and neighbors came to call she stayed in her room upstairs. But she always kept her door open so she could hear what was going on. It was around this time that she started to wear only white.

The more Emily stayed by herself, the more curious people in town became about her. Some made up stories about Emily to explain her odd ways. Others came to the door with little gifts just to see if they could get a glimpse of Emily. But Emily saw only those she chose to see. Vinnie always talked to visitors, but protected Emily from the curious. The family did not understand Emily's need to be away from the world, but they respected her wishes.

Her nieces and nephews and the neighborhood children didn't seem to mind that Emily was different. They loved to play in her yard. Sometimes she worked in the garden and watched them from there or the window. When Emily waved her arms to signal, play stopped. Then she would open the window and lower a basket, filled with warm gingerbread, cookies, or raisins, by a knotted cord. Her nephew Ned called Emily his best friend. And once, when her niece, Mattie, was angry with a playmate, Mattie yelled the worst thing she could think of: "You haven't got an Aunt Emily!"

Over the years Emily taught herself to write poetry by writing and writing and writing. After most people had gone to bed, Emily sat up writing. Emily wrote extraordinary things; she lived "in Possibility." Sunrises, sunsets, the moon, shadows on the lawn, storms, and bees were in her poems. But the sun didn't just rise; it rose "a ribbon at a time." The moon could show "a chin of gold," or slide down a chair. A sunset wasn't just pretty colors; it was a woman sweeping with many brooms, each a different color that left a few shreds, or straws, behind. Hills could untie bonnets. With Emily's imagination, lightning displayed a yellow beak and ugly blue claws. A maple tree wore a gay scarf. Birds didn't fly; they unrolled their feathers and rowed home. Her poems about flowers, butterflies, and bees reveal the delight she took in nature and her keen sense of the funny side of things. A good example is her letter from Fly to Bee (see page 31).

Only six of Emily's poems were published while she was alive. Her poems were unusual, not what people seemed to like at the time. Poetry in those days was serious and often used "flowery" language. Emily's was light and witty.

She almost always wrote in a rhythm or meter called iambic. It is supposed to be most like ordinary speech, and is the rhythm used in many of the hymns Emily sang in church. A short syllable is followed by a long one. You can usually clap the rhythm of her poems. The first clap is soft, or weak, and the second loud, or strong. Turn to the poem on page 20 and try it.

Her poems often have stanzas of four lines. In these poems, lines one and three have eight syllables, lines two and four have six syllables, and the last word in line two rhymes with the last word in line four. For an example, see the poem on page 34 entitled "The bee is not afraid of me." Most of her poems have two stanzas, but sometimes there are more; in these poems, each stanza follows the pattern set in the first stanza.

Writing a poem according to these rules is like working out a puzzle. Emily would think of what she wanted to say, then work until it fit the pattern. She always kept a dictionary beside her so she could find a word that would say exactly what she wanted. Many times she marked through a word and replaced it with another. Sometimes she broke the "rules" to include a word that didn't quite fit or to play with an idea in a different way. People were shocked by this, for it was not what they expected.

Almost every evening, Emily sent a note, and often a poem, to Austin's wife, Sue, such as "The morns are meeker than they were" on page 40. Like Ben Newton, Sue was interested in Emily's poetry, although not even Sue knew how much Emily had written. After Emily died at age fifty-five, Vinnie went into her room. To Vinnie's great surprise, she found in the bottom drawer of Emily's bureau a box of little books, each sewn together by hand. There were 879 poems in the little books. Later, more poems were found, for odd little Emily had written more than seventeen hundred poems!

Why did she write? We may never know for certain. But we do know this; Emily Dickinson chose to spend day after day in the same house, doing the same things—ordinary, seemingly unimportant things—for she seemed to know that there are wonderful possibilities in the most ordinary life if we just take notice.

Emily wrote in a letter, "To live is so startling it leaves little time for anything else." Living, thinking, and imagining were a full-time job to Emily Dickinson. She believed that feelings are to be thought about, not put aside. Perhaps she wrote to capture what she noticed, what she imagined, and how she felt.

Hope is the thing with feathers
That perches in the soul,
And sings the tune without the words,
And never stops at all,

And sweetest in the gale is heard;
And sore must be the storm
That could abash the little bird
That kept so many warm.

I've heard it in the chillest land,
And on the strangest sea;
Yet, never, in extremity,
It asked a crumb of me.

gale—*a strong wind*
abash—*to astonish; to make feel ill at
        ease or self-conscious*
extremity—*a most difficult or dangerous
        time or situation*

It's all I have to bring today,
　　This, and my heart beside,
This, and my heart, and all the fields,
　　And all the meadows wide.
Be sure you count, should I forget—
　　Some one the sum could tell—
This, and my heart, and all the bees
　　Which in the clover dwell.

I started early, took my dog,
And visited the sea—
The mermaids in the basement
Came out to look at me,

And frigates in the upper floor
Extended hempen hands—
Presuming me to be a mouse
Aground, upon the sands,

But no man moved me till the tide
Went past my simple shoe—
And past my apron and my belt,
And past my bodice too,

And made as he would eat me up
And wholly as a dew
Upon a dandelion's sleeve—
And then I started too.

And he—he followed close behind;
I felt his silver heel
Upon my ankle—then my shoes
Would overflow with pearl.

Until we met the solid town,
No one he seemed to know—
And bowing with a mighty look
At me, the sea withdrew.

frigates—*medium-sized warships with sails*
hempen—*ropelike (some rope is made from hemp, which is a*
  plant with tough fiber in its stem)
bodice—*the part of a woman's dress above the waist*

I'm nobody! Who are you?
Are you nobody, too?
Then there's a pair of us—don't tell!
They'd banish us, you know.

How dreary to be somebody!
How public, like a frog
To tell your name the livelong day
To an admiring bog!

banish—*to send away or get rid of*
bog—*wet, marshy ground*

I hide myself within my flower,
That wearing on your breast
You, unsuspecting, wear me too—
And angels know the rest.

I hide myself within my flower,
That fading from your vase,
You, unsuspecting, feel for me
Almost a loneliness.

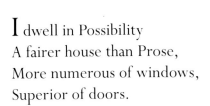

I dwell in Possibility
A fairer house than Prose,
More numerous of windows,
Superior of doors.

Of chambers, as the cedars—
Impregnable of eye;
And for an everlasting roof
The gables of the sky.

Of visitors—the fairest—
For occupation—this—
The spreading wide my narrow hands
To gather Paradise.

impregnable—*can't be captured; unshakable*

Will there really be a morning?
Is there such a thing as day?
Could I see it from the mountains
If I were as tall as they?

Has it feet like water-lilies?
Has it feathers like a bird?
Is it brought from famous countries
Of which I have never heard?

Oh, some scholar! Oh, some sailor!
Oh, some wise man from the skies!
Please to tell a little pilgrim
Where the place called morning lies!

I'll tell you how the sun rose,—
A ribbon at a time.
The steeples swam in amethyst,
The news like squirrels ran.

The hills untied their bonnets,
The bobolinks begun.
Then I said softly to myself,
"That must have been the sun!"

But how he set I know not.
There seemed a purple stile
Which little yellow boys and girls
Were climbing all the while

Till when they reached the other side,
A dominie in gray
Put gently up the evening bars,
And led the flock away.

amethyst—*purple or violet color; a kind of
        quartz used in jewelry*
bobolinks—*songbirds that live in fields and
        meadows*
stile—*a set of steps used for climbing over
        a fence or wall*
dominie—*a pastor or member of the clergy;
        in Scotland, a schoolmaster*

She sweeps with many-colored brooms,
And leaves the shreds behind;
Oh, housewife in the evening west,
Come back, and dust the pond!

You dropped a purple ravelling in,
You dropped an amber thread;
And now you've littered all the East
With duds of emerald!

And still she plies her spotted brooms,
And still the aprons fly,
Till brooms fade softly into stars—
And then I come away.

ravelling—*a thread that has been pulled from
a woven cloth*
plies—*uses energetically*

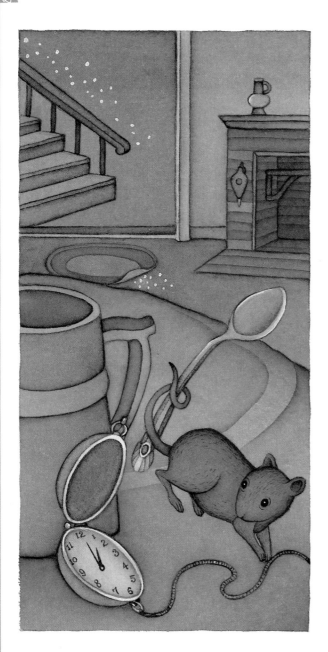

I know some lonely houses off the road
A robber'd like the look of.—
Wooden-barred,
And windows hanging low,
Inviting to
A portico,
Where two could creep:
One hand the tools,
The other peep
To make sure all's asleep.
Old-fashioned eyes,
Not easy to surprise!

How orderly the kitchen'd look by night,
With just a clock,—
But they could gag the tick,
And mice won't bark;
And so the walls don't tell,
None will.

A pair of spectacles ajar just stir—
An almanac's aware.
Was it the mat winked,
Or a nervous star?
The moon slides down the stair
To see who's there.

There's plunder,—where?
Tankard, or spoon,
Earring, or stone,
A watch, some ancient brooch
To match the grandmamma,
Staid sleeping there.

Day rattles, too,
Stealth's slow;
The sun has got as far
As the third sycamore.
Screams chanticleer,
"Who's there?"
And echoes, trains away,
Sneer—"Where?"
While the old couple, just astir,
Fancy the sunrise left the door ajar!

portico—*a porch or covered walk that has a*
roof supported by columns; often at
the entrance to a building
plunder—*a stolen item*
stealth—*secret, sly action*
chanticleer—*an ancient name for a rooster*

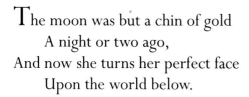The moon was but a chin of gold
    A night or two ago,
And now she turns her perfect face
    Upon the world below.

Her forehead is of amplest blonde,
    Her cheek like beryl stone,
Her eye unto the summer dew
    The likest I have known.

Her lips of amber never part,
    But what must be the smile
Upon her friend she could bestow,
    Were such her silver will.

And what a privilege to be
    But the remotest star.
For certainly her way might pass
    Beside your twinkling door.

Her bonnet is the firmament,
    The universe her shoe,
The stars the trinkets at her belt,
    Her dimities of blue.

Pink, small, and punctual
Aromatic, low,
Covert in April,
Candid in May,

Dear to the moss,
Known by the knoll,
Next to the robin
In every human soul,

Bold little beauty,
Bedecked with thee,
Nature forswears Antiquity.

covert—*hidden or disguised*
knoll—*a little hill or mound*

(an arbutus, a plant with little pink or white blossoms and strawberry-like berries)

His bill an auger is,
His head, a cap and frill.
He laboreth at every tree,—
A worm his utmost goal.

auger—*a tool for drilling holes in wood*

(a woodpecker)

An everywhere of silver,
With ropes of sand
To keep it from effacing
The track called land.

effacing—*wiping out or erasing something*

(the sea)

121

I like to see it lap the miles,
And lick the valleys up,
And stop to feed itself at tanks;
And then, prodigious, step

Around a pile of mountains,
And, supercilious, peer
In shanties by the sides of roads;
And then a quarry pare

To fit its sides, and crawl between,
Complaining all the while
In horrid, hooting stanza;
Then chase itself down hill

And neigh like Boanerges;
Then, punctual as a star,
Stop—docile and omnipotent—
At its own stable door.

prodigious—*amazing; of great size and power*
supercilious—*haughty or proud*
shanties—*small, shabby huts or houses*
quarry—*a place where stone or marble used for building is cut or blasted out of the ground*
Boanerges—*the Apostles James and John, who were called the "Sons of Thunder" because they wanted to call down fire from heaven on the Samaritans (see Mark 3:17)*
omnipotent—*all-powerful*

(a train)

A fuzzy fellow without feet
Yet doth exceeding run!
Of velvet is his countenance
And his complexion dun.

Sometimes he dwelleth in the grass,
Sometimes upon a bough
From which he doth descend in plush
Upon the passer-by.

dun—*a dull grayish brown*

(a caterpillar who becomes a butterfly)

124

It sifts from leaden sieves,
It powders all the wood,
It fills with alabaster wool
The wrinkles of the road.

It makes an even face
Of mountain and of plain,—
Unbroken forehead from the east
Unto the east again.

It reaches to the fence,
It wraps it, rail by rail,
Till it is lost in fleeces;
It flings a crystal veil

On stump and stack and stem,—
The summer's empty room,
Acres of seams where harvests were,
Recordless, but for them.

It ruffles wrists of posts,
And ankles of a queen,—
Then stills its artisans like ghosts,
Denying they have been.

(ᴍous)

sieves—*strainers or sifters*
artisans—*skilled workers or craftspeople who make things that show imagination and feeling*

A narrow fellow in the grass
Occasionally rides;
You may have met him,—did you not,
His notice sudden is.

The grass divides as with a comb,
A spotted shaft is seen;
And then it closes at your feet
And opens further on.

He likes a boggy acre,
A floor to cool for corn.
Yet when a child, and barefoot,
I more than once, at morn,

Have passed, I thought, a whip-lash
Unbraiding in the sun,—
When, stooping to secure it,
It wrinkled, and was gone.

Several of nature's people
I know, and they know me;
I feel for them a transport
Of cordiality;

But never met this fellow,
Attended or alone,
Without a tighter breathing,
And zero at the bone.

(a snake)

Dear March, come in!
How glad I am!
I looked for you before.
Put down your hat—
You must have walked—
How out of breath you are!
Dear March, how are you?
And the rest?
Did you leave Nature well?
Oh, March, come right upstairs with me,
I have so much to tell!

I got your letter, and the birds'—
The maples never knew
That you were coming—I declare,
How red their faces grew!
But, March, forgive me—
And all those hills
You left for me to hue—
There was no purple suitable,
You took it all with you.

Who knocks? That April!
Lock the door!
I will not be pursued!
He stayed away a year, to call
When I am occupied.
But trifles look so trivial
As soon as you have come,
That blame is just as dear as praise
And praise as mere as blame.

hue—*a particular color or tint
(Emily is saying, "You left
it up to me to put the color in!")*

128

Bee, I'm expecting you!
Was saying yesterday
To somebody you know
That you were due.

The frogs got home last week,
Are settled and at work,
Birds mostly back,
The clover warm and thick.

You'll get my letter by
The seventeenth; reply,
Or better, be with me.
      Yours,
         Fly.

The grass so little has to do,
A sphere of simple green
With only butterflies to brood
And bees to entertain.

And stir all day to pretty tunes
The breezes fetch along
And hold the sunshine in its lap
And bow to everything.

And thread the dews all night, like pearls,
And make itself so fine—
A duchess were too common
For such a noticing.

And even when it dies, to pass
In odors so divine,
As lowly spices gone to sleep,
Or amulets of pine.

And then to dwell in sovereign barns,
And dream the days away—
The grass so little has to do,
I wish I were a hay!

sovereign—*superior to every other; the best,
greatest, or most important*

A bird came down the walk—
He did not know I saw;
He bit an angleworm in halves
And ate the fellow, raw.

And then he drank a dew
From a convenient grass,
And then hopped sidewise to the wall
To let a beetle pass.

He glanced with rapid eyes
That hurried all abroad—
They looked like frightened beads, I thought—
He stirred his velvet head—

Like one in danger; cautious,
I offered him a crumb,
And he unrolled his feathers
And rowed him softer home

Than oars divide the ocean,
Too silver for a seam,
Or butterflies, off banks of noon,
Leap, plashless, as they swim.

plashless—*without splashing*

The bee is not afraid of me,
I know the butterfly,
The pretty people in the woods
Receive me cordially.

The brooks laugh louder when I come,
The breezes madder play.
Wherefore, mine eyes, thy silver mists?
Wherefore, O summer's day?

A soft sea washed around the house,
A sea of summer air,
And rose and fell the magic planks
That sailed without a care.

For captain was the butterfly,
For helmsman was the bee,
And an entire universe
For the delighted crew.

To make a prairie it takes a clover and one bee—
One clover, and a bee,
And revery.
The revery alone will do
If bees are few.

revery—*dreamy thinking; a state in which
one imagines pleasant things*

The pedigree of honey
Does not conern the bee—
A clover, any time to him
Is aristocracy.

Forbidden fruit a flavor has
    That lawful orchards mocks;
How luscious lies the pea within
    The pod that Duty locks!

The wind begun to rock the grass
With threatening tunes and low,—
He flung a menace at the earth,
A menace at the sky.

The leaves unhooked themselves from trees
And started all abroad;
The dust did scoop itself like hands
And throw away the road.

The wagons quickened on the streets,
The thunder hurried slow;
The lightning showed a yellow beak,
And then a livid claw.

The birds put up the bars to nests,
The cattle fled to barns;
There came one drop of giant rain,
And then, as if the hands

That held the dams had parted hold,
The waters wrecked the sky,
But overlooked my father's house,
Just quartering a tree.

livid—*having a bluish color; black-and-blue;
discolored by a bruise*

The morns are meeker than they were,
The nuts are getting brown;
The berry's cheek is plumper,
The rose is out of town.

The maple wears a gayer scarf,
The field a scarlet gown.
Lest I should be old-fashioned,
I'll put a trinket on.

I have not told my garden yet,
Lest that should conquer me;
I have not quite the strength now
To break it to the bee.

I will not name it in the street,
For shops would stare, that I,
So shy, so very ignorant,
Should have the face to die.

The hillsides must not know it,
Where I have rambled so,
Nor tell the loving forests
The day that I shall go,

Nor lisp it at the table,
Nor heedless by the way
Hint that within the riddle
One will walk to-day!

My river runs to thee—
Blue sea, wilt welcome me?

My river waits reply.
Oh sea, look graciously!

I'll fetch thee brooks
From spotted nooks—

Say, sea,
Take me!

I never saw a moor,
I never saw the sea,
Yet know I how the heather looks,
And what a wave must be.

I never spoke with God,
Nor visited in heaven,
Yet certain am I of the spot
As if the chart were given.

There is no frigate like a book
    To take us lands away,
Nor any coursers like a page
    Of prancing poetry.
This traverse may the poorest take
    Without oppress of toll;
How frugal is the chariot
    That bears a human soul!

frigate—*a medium-sized warship with sails*
coursers—*graceful, swift horses or runners*

If I can stop one heart from breaking,
I shall not live in vain;
If I can ease one life the aching,
Or cool one pain,
Or help one fainting robin
Unto his nest again,
I shall not live in vain.

A word is dead
When it is said,
 Some say.
I say it just
Begins to live
 That day.

In this short life
That only lasts an hour,
How much, how little,
Is within our power!

Edgar Allan Poe

Edited by Brod Bagert
Illustrated by Carolynn Cobleigh

Introduction

MANY OF THE POEMS OF EDGAR ALLAN POE, "ANNABEL Lee" and "The Raven" in particular, are marked by deep sadness over the loss of a loved one. It is a sadness that began in Poe's childhood with his father's desertion and the death of his mother—a dark sadness that continued throughout his life.

In the early 1800s, Americans began to notice a beautiful young actress named Eliza Poe. She was married to David Poe, also an actor, and they had a son, William. Between 1806 and 1809, Eliza's and David's lives were changed by three important events. First, Eliza became a rising star in Boston. Theatergoers loved her beautiful and powerful presence onstage. Then, during the stormy winter of 1809, Eliza gave birth to a second son, Edgar. Finally, in that same year, the people at the Park Street Theater in New York, at the time America's largest and most famous theater, wooed the Poes to their stage. This was the break the Poes had been hoping for, so they moved to New York City.

New York audiences received Eliza with enthusiasm and affection, and it was apparent that she would soon be one of the most famous actresses in America. But her husband had little experience as an actor and, according to New York theater critics, even less talent. He missed performances because of "a sudden illness," which was really drunkenness. After only six weeks, David Poe deserted his wife and two sons and was never heard from again.

Eliza was left to care for her sons while she pursued her acting career. In December 1810, she gave birth to a girl, Rosalie. Although Eliza returned to the stage in the summer of 1811, she was very ill. She was bedridden by October and never performed again. Two months later, Eliza Poe said her last farewell to her children. Edgar was not yet three years old.

John and Frances Allan lived in Richmond, Virginia, and were avid theatergoers. Frances had helped care for Mrs. Poe and had become quite fond of little Edgar. The Allans had no children, so they decided to take Edgar in when his mother died, while William was sent to live with relatives in Baltimore and Rosalie was taken in by another Richmond family. Although he was never formally adopted, Poe lived with the Allans for a long time, and he honored them by taking Allan as his middle name.

John Allan was an independent, self-made merchant who believed in perseverance, hard work, and commitment to duty. He had a reputation for social benevolence, but was also a strict taskmaster. Frances was a dedicated homemaker, and she provided well for Poe. The Allans made sure that he received the benefits of an education, mostly at boarding schools. Allan said that by age six Poe was a "good scholar" and that he had learned to read Latin "pretty sharply." By age thirteen, Poe read the Latin poets with fluency, and he began to write poetry of his own. He also excelled in athletics: he was a good boxer, a fast runner, and an exceptional swimmer. He once swam six miles in the James River, and he set a school broad-jump record of 21 feet 6 inches.

Although Poe seemed happy, deep inside he was confused. Because he was never formally adopted, he felt uncertain about his position in the Allan family, and his doubt often made him cross and dejected. Allan interpreted Poe's behavior as a lack of gratitude. When Poe was sixteen and entering the University of Virginia, resentments between Poe and Allan were simmering beneath the surface.

While in college, Poe wrote his first story. Although most of Poe's stories are rather gloomy, this one was bright and funny. When he read the story to his friends, however, they teased him about it, so he threw it into the fire. Eventually, Poe learned to accept criticism—but it was too late to save his first story.

Poe was an excellent student, but he accumulated large debts. He claimed that Allan did not give him enough money and asked for more. Allan blamed Poe's lack of money on his drinking, gambling, and expensive tastes. At the end of his first year in college, Poe was several thousand dollars in debt, which Allan refused to pay. As a result, Poe could not return to college.

Poe returned to his birthplace and got a job, using his spare time to write poetry. There he published his first book, *Tamerlane and Other Poems*, but did not use his name, saying instead that it was written by "a Bostonian." By the time the book appeared, he had enlisted in the army. He was eighteen and a minor, so he should have obtained John Allan's consent to join. However, he did not want to tell Allan of his plans, so he enlisted under the name Edgar A. Perry and said he was twenty-two.

Poe did well in the army. A lieutenant said that he performed his duties "promptly and faithfully" and that he was "entirely free from drinking." On New Year's Day, 1829, Poe was made a sergeant major, the highest rank for a noncommissioned officer. But Poe was unhappy, so he told the truth about his age and requested an early discharge. The lieutenant agreed only if Poe would reconcile with John Allan. Poe sent Allan three letters, but Allan ignored them until eventually, softened by the death of his wife, he agreed to the reconciliation.

Poe had planned to be discharged so that he could attend the U.S. Military Academy at West Point. It took him a year to gain admission, and during that time he continued to write poetry. In November 1829, he published *Al Aaraaf*, using his real name. Although the book received mixed reviews, it did not go unnoticed.

About this time Poe and Allan began to quarrel again. Allan continued to provide less money than Poe thought he needed. Allan remarried, which made Poe feel rejected. Poe decided to leave West Point, but Allan refused to sign the required resignation papers, so Poe vowed that he would get himself dishonorably discharged, which he did in January 1831. After that, Poe and Allan had little contact, and when Allan died in 1834, there was no mention of Poe in his will.

After leaving West Point, Poe lived in New York for two years. There he published a new book that received little notice, much of it unfavorable. Hungry and disappointed, he went to Baltimore to live with his widowed aunt, Maria Poe Clemm, who was already caring for Poe's brother, William, an alcoholic. William died a few months later, leaving Poe alone with Maria and her daughter, Virginia.

In 1834 Poe got a job in Baltimore with a magazine, first as a contributor (in a single year he contributed eighty-three reviews, four essays, six poems, and three stories) and eventually as an editor. Poe made the magazine one of the nation's most respected publications. But three years later, he was fired because his alcoholism interfered with his job. It was obvious that Poe could no longer control his drinking. While sober, Poe wrote the words that made him famous, but he could not stop drinking completely. Poe once wrote to a friend, "During these long fits of absolute unconsciousness I drank—God only knows how often or how much."

Poe's frustration with his addiction is reflected in his story "The Cask of Amontillado," in which a victim is lured by his murderer's promise of a drink of wine into dark underground passages. The murderer places the victim in chains and begins to seal him behind a brick wall. As he places the last brick, the victim screams out for the wine he was promised. As in the story, Poe's addiction led him into dark places.

In 1837, Poe, age twenty-seven, married his first cousin Virginia, age thirteen, perhaps to secure his place in the Clemm household. Two years later, Poe's first collection of short stories, *Tales of the Grotesque and Arabesque,* was published. While some thought it was particularly gloomy, the book was generally received as the most powerful collection of short fiction ever published in America. Unfortunately, it was published during a recession, so only seven hundred fifty copies were printed, and those took three years to sell. Although Poe was becoming more famous, he was still poor, and both he and his wife were ill.

Poe's skill as a storyteller continued to grow. In 1841, he penned a detective story called "The Murders in the Rue Morgue." Although detective stories are common today, Poe wrote the first one, inventing a new literary form. In 1845, *The Raven and Other Poems* was published, a collection that includes "The Raven," one of the most popular poems ever written.

The Poes were married for ten years until, after a long illness, Virginia passed away. After she died, Poe collapsed and was nursed back to health by Marie Louise Shew, who inspired "The Beloved Physician," the lost poem of which a part appears in this book.

Poe once wrote that "the death of a beautiful woman is, unquestionably, the most poetical topic in the world." It is a topic that Poe knew all too well: in his short lifetime, he had lost his mother, his foster mother, and his wife. There is little wonder why so many of his poems are about the death of a loved one.

In the years that followed, Poe pursued a number of women. In each instance, either his reputation or his drinking kept the women from marrying him. At one point, he even returned to Richmond and became reacquainted with his old girlfriend, Elmira Royster, who was now wealthy and recently widowed. On September 27, 1849, he left Richmond for Baltimore, the first stop on a business trip. No one knows what went on during the next week of Poe's life. On October 3, a printer named Joseph Walker noticed Poe, whom he described as "rather worse for wear," in a Baltimore tavern. Walker immediately notified a friend of Poe's, Joseph Snodgrass, who promptly had Poe admitted to a hospital.

For days Poe slipped in and out of consciousness. Just when he seemed to be improving, his condition would take a turn for the worse. He became delirious, ranting and raving for several hours. At three o'clock on the morning of Sunday, October 7, 1849, Poe said, "Lord help my poor soul!" and died. He was only forty years old.

Edgar Allan Poe was a master storyteller and a great poet. Three of his poems, "Annabel Lee," "The Raven," and "The Bells," are among the most beautiful and moving poems in the English language. All three were written in the last five years of his life. Like his mother, Poe was brilliantly talented. Like his father, Poe was destroyed by alcoholism. Sadly, Poe died when he was just beginning to achieve his full power as a great poet.

A NOTE TO PARENTS

What we have done in this volume is a little unusual, and we'd like to explain why and how we did it. You will not find the last eight "poems" in this book in any of Poe's other collections. This is because Poe did not actually write them as poems; they were originally part of larger prose works.

Beautiful poetic passages can often be found in longer prose works. These powerful moments gleam like diamonds in the silver setting of the surrounding prose. Such gems are often the poetic equal of the author's "official" poems. This seems especially true of nineteenth-century American writers, and Poe is no exception. So we searched his stories to find passages which, although published as prose, stand out as poetry. The idea is to give the full range of Poe's poetic voice, so children can feel the full power of his poetry.

When we found one of these passages, we faced the task of presenting it in poetic form. This required us to "tinker" with the work of a great writer, so we were as delicate as possible. While some words and phrases were omitted and the text was rearranged into verses, what remains is entirely the work of Edgar Allan Poe. But still we wondered: "Would Mr. Poe have approved?"

We decided he would. Poe believed a poem was a communication between the poet and the reader, and he put the needs of the reader first. In his essay "The Poetic Principle," he wrote, "A poem deserves its title only inasmuch as it excites, by elevating the soul." Since Poe defined poetry in terms of its ability to excite the soul of the reader, we think he would probably approve of our approach. We suspect that he might even feel gratified to know that, in this way, the children of our generation can hear the full beauty of his poetic voice and come to love his poetry.

ALONE

When we read this poem we learn that since his childhood Poe had believed he was different from other people. This belief made him feel lonely, and his loneliness was like a "demon" that he saw everywhere he turned.

From childhood's hour I have not been
As others were—I have not seen
As others saw—I could not bring
My passions from a common spring—
From the same source I have not taken
My sorrow—I could not awaken
My heart to joy at the same tone—
And all I ever lov'd—I lov'd alone—
Then—in my childhood—in the dawn
Of a most stormy life—was drawn
From every depth of good and ill
The mystery which binds me still—
From the torrent, or the fountain—
From the red cliff of the mountain—
From the sun that 'round me roll'd
In its autumn tint of gold—
From the lightning in the sky
As it pass'd me flying by—
From the thunder, and the storm—
And the cloud that took the form
(When the rest of Heaven was blue)
Of a demon in my view—

torrent–*flood of water*

ANNABEL LEE

In this poem a man tells of his love for a girl named Annabel Lee. The poem is happy at first, but turns sad when we learn that Annabel Lee has died. Then we realize that the man has gone mad when he accuses the angels of killing Annabel Lee out of jealousy. This is a great poem to read out loud, for in it Poe has made the English language sound very musical.

It was many and many a year ago,
    In a kingdom by the sea,
That a maiden there lived whom you may know
    By the name of Annabel Lee;
And this maiden she lived with no other thought
    Than to love and be loved by me.

I was a child and *she* was a child,
    In this kingdom by the sea:
But we loved with a love that was more than love—
    I and my Annabel Lee;
With a love that the winged seraphs of heaven
    Coveted her and me.

---

seraphs–*angels*   coveted–*wanted to take from*

And this was the reason that, long ago,
   In this kingdom by the sea.
A wind blew out of a cloud, chilling
   My beautiful Annabel Lee;
So that her high-born kinsmen came
   And bore her away from me,
To shut her up in a sepulchre
   In this kingdom by the sea.

The angels, not half so happy in heaven,
   Went envying her and me—
Yes!—that was the reason (as all men know,
   In this kingdom by the sea)
That the wind came out of the cloud by night,
   Chilling and killing my Annabel Lee.

But our love it was stronger by far than the love
   Of those who were older than we—
   Of many far wiser than we—
And neither the angels in heaven above,
   Nor the demons down under the sea,
Can ever dissever my soul from the soul
   Of the beautiful Annabel Lee,

For the moon never beams without bringing me dreams
   Of the beautiful Annabel Lee;
And the stars never rise but I feel the bright eyes
Of the beautiful Annabel Lee;
And so, all the night-tide, I lie down by the side
Of my darling—my darling—my life and my bride,
    In the sepulchre there by the sea,
    In her tomb by the sounding sea.

---

sepulchre–*tomb* dissever–*separate*

THE LAKE

The "lake" described in this poem is the Lake of the Dismal Swamp, which Poe visited as a young man. Legend holds that the lake is haunted by the ghosts of two lovers. A young man, unable to accept the death of the girl he loved, imagined that she was alive somewhere in the swamp, followed her there, and was never seen again.

In this poem, Poe describes how he felt when visiting the lake—how he found it beautiful by day but scary at night. Yet even as a child, Poe was delighted by the "terror."

In youth's spring, it was my lot
To haunt of the wide earth a spot
The which I could not love the less;
So lovely was the loneliness
Of a wild lake, with black rock bound,
And the tall pines that tower'd around.

But when the night had thrown her pall
Upon that spot—as upon all,
And the wind would pass me by
In its still melody,
My infant spirit would awake
To the terror of that lone lake.

Yet that terror was not fright—
But a tremulous delight,
And a feeling undefin'd
Springing from a darken'd mind.

Death was in that poison'd wave
And in its gulf a fitting grave
For him who thence could solace bring
To his dark imagining;
Whose wild'ring thought could even make
An Eden of that dim lake.

---

pall–*cloth covering a coffin* tremulous–*affected with trembling* solace–*comfort* wild'ring–*bewildering*

THE RAVEN

This is probably Poe's most famous poem. "The Raven" is a great poem to read out loud. It's a bit long, but with some practice you can read it with the kind of expression that will give your friends goosebumps.

The poem opens on a man alone in his house. He is very sad over the death of Lenore, the woman he loved, and he is reading to relieve his sorrow. He hears what he thinks is a person knocking at his door. Eventually he learns that it is not a person at all but a bird—a raven. At first he is amused, but soon grows sad. The bird can say only one word, "Nevermore," and that word reminds him that nothing can bring back his lost Lenore.

Once upon a midnight dreary, while I pondered, weak and weary,
Over many a quaint and curious volume of forgotten lore—
While I nodded, nearly napping, suddenly there came a tapping,
As of some one gently rapping, rapping at my chamber door.
"'Tis some visitor," I muttered, "tapping at my chamber door—
    Only this and nothing more."

Ah, distinctly I remember it was in the bleak December;
And each separate dying ember wrought its ghost upon the floor.
Eagerly I wished the morrow;—vainly I had sought to borrow
From my books surcease of sorrow—sorrow for the lost Lenore—
For the rare and radiant maiden whom the angels name Lenore—
    Nameless here for evermore.

And the silken, sad, uncertain rustling of each purple curtain
Thrilled me—filled me with fantastic terrors never felt before;
So that now, to still the beating of my heart, I stood repeating
"'Tis some visitor entreating entrance at my chamber door—
Some late visitor entreating entrance at my chamber door;—
    This it is and nothing more."

Presently my soul grew stronger; hesitating then no longer,
"Sir," said I, "or Madam, truly your forgiveness I implore;
But the fact is I was napping, and so gently you came rapping,
And so faintly you came tapping, tapping at my chamber door,
That I scarce was sure I heard you"—here I opened wide the door;—
    Darkness there and nothing more.

---

lore–*legend* surcease–*an end* entreating–*requesting*

Deep into that darkness peering, long I stood there wondering, fearing,
Doubting, dreaming dreams no mortal ever dared to dream before;
But the silence was unbroken, and the stillness gave no token,
And the only word there spoken was the whispered word, "Lenore!"
This I whispered, and an echo murmured back the word "Lenore!"
    Merely this and nothing more.

Back into the chamber turning, all my soul within me burning,
Soon again I heard a tapping somewhat louder than before.
"Surely," said I, "surely that is something at my window lattice;
Let me see, then what thereat is, and this mystery explore—
Let my heart be still a moment and this mystery explore;—
    'Tis the wind and nothing more!"

Open here I flung the shutter, when with many a flirt and flutter
In there stepped a stately Raven of the saintly days of yore;
Not the least obeisance made he; not a minute stopped or stayed he;
But, with mien of lord or lady, perched above my chamber door—
Perched upon a bust of Pallas just above my chamber door—
    Perched, and sat, and nothing more.

Then this ebony bird beguiling my sad fancy into smiling,
But the grave and stern decorum of the countenance it wore,
"Though thy crest be shorn and shaven, thou," I said, "art sure no craven,
Ghastly grim and ancient Raven wandering from the Nightly shore—
Tell me what thy lordly name is on the Night's Plutonian shore!"
    Quoth the Raven, "Nevermore."

Much I marveled this ungainly fowl to hear discourse so plainly,
Though its answer little meaning—little relevancy bore;
For we cannot help agreeing that no living human being
Ever yet was blessed with seeing bird above his chamber door—
Bird or beast upon the sculptured bust above his chamber door,
    With such name as "Nevermore."

token–*clue*   lattice–*window covering made from strips of crossed wood*   yore–*long ago*
obeisance–*sign of obedience*   mien–*appearance*   Pallas–*Athena, goddess of wisdom*
ebony–*black*   beguiling–*charming*   decorum–*dignity*   countenance–*facial expression*   craven–*coward*
Plutonian–*deathly*   ungainly–*clumsy*   discourse–*speech*   relevancy–*importance*

But the Raven, sitting lonely on that placid bust, spoke only
That one word, as if his soul in that one word he did outpour.
Nothing further then he uttered—not a feather then he fluttered—
Till I scarcely more than muttered, "Other friends have flown before—
On the morrow *he* will leave me, as my hopes have flown before."
    Then the bird said "Nevermore."

Startled at the stillness broken by reply so aptly spoken,
"Doubtless," said I, "what it utters is its only stock and store
Caught from some unhappy master whom unmerciful Disaster
Followed fast and followed faster till his songs one burden bore—
Till the dirges of his Hope the melancholy burden bore
    Of 'Never—nevermore.'"

But the Raven still beguiling my sad fancy into smiling,
Straight I wheeled a cushioned seat in front of bird, and bust and door;
Then, upon the velvet sinking, I betook myself to linking
Fancy unto fancy, thinking what this ominous bird of yore—
What this grim, ungainly, ghastly, gaunt, and ominous bird of yore
    Meant in croaking "Nevermore."

This I sat engaged in guessing, but no syllable expressing
To the fowl whose fiery eyes now burned into my bosom's core;
This and more I sat divining, with my head at ease reclining
On the cushion's velvet lining that the lamp-light gloated o'er,
But whose velvet violet lining with the lamp-light gloating o'er,
    She shall press, ah, nevermore!

Then, methought, the air grew denser, perfumed from an unseen censer
Swung by Seraphim whose foot-falls tinkled on the tufted floor.
"Wretch," I cried, "thy God hath lent thee—by these angels he hath sent thee
Respite—respite and nepenthe from thy memories of Lenore;
Quaff, oh quaff this kind nepenthe and forget this lost Lenore!"
    Quoth the Raven "Nevermore."

---

dirges –*burial songs*   ominous–*spooky*   divining–*coming to a conclusion*   denser–*thicker*
censer–*incense burner*   seraphim–*angel*   nepenthe–*drink that causes forgetfulness*   quaff–*to drink*

"Prophet!" said I, "thing of evil!—prophet still, if bird or devil!—
Whether Tempter sent, or whether tempest tossed thee here ashore,
Desolate yet all undaunted, on this desert land enchanted—
On this home by Horror haunted—tell me truly, I implore—
Is there—*is* there balm in Gilead?—tell me—tell me, I implore!"
    Quoth the Raven "Nevermore."

"Prophet!" said I, "thing of evil!—prophet still, if bird or devil!
By that Heaven that bends above us—by that God we both adore—
Tell this soul with sorrow laden if, within the distant Aidenn,
It shall clasp a sainted maiden whom the angels name Lenore—
Clasp a rare and radiant maiden whom the angels name Lenore."
    Quoth the Raven "Nevermore."

"Be that word our sign of parting, bird or fiend!" I shrieked, upstarting—
"Get thee back into the tempest and the Night's Plutonian shore!
Leave no black plume as a token of that lie thy soul hath spoken!
Leave my loneliness unbroken!—quit the bust above my door!
Take thy beak from out my heart, and take thy form from off my door!"
    Quoth the Raven "Nevermore."

And the Raven, never flitting, still is sitting, *still* is sitting
On the pallid bust of Pallas just above my chamber door;
And his eyes have all the seeming of a demon's that is dreaming,
And the lamp-light o'er him streaming throws his shadow on the floor;
And my soul from out that shadow that lies floating on the floor
    Shall be lifted—nevermore!

tempter–*devil* tempest–*storm* desolate–*alone* undaunted–*unafraid* balm–*soothing oil*
Gilead–*ancient place in the Middle East known for its balm* Aidenn–*Aidin, a rich province of Turkey*
plume–*feather* pallid–*pale*

TO HELEN

This is a romantic poem in the voice of a man who is standing outside the house of a woman named Helen. It is nighttime. Helen, holding an oil lamp, steps in front of the window. We suspect that she is signaling to someone. The man outside, very happy to see her, tells us that Helen's beauty is like a ship sent to bring him home from the sea.

Helen, thy beauty is to me
    Like those Nicaean barks of yore,
That gently, o'er a perfumed sea,
    The weary, way-worn wanderer bore
    To his own native shore.

On desperate seas long wont to roam,
    Thy hyacinth hair, thy classic face,
Thy Naiad airs have brought me home
    To the glory that was Greece,
    And the grandeur that was Rome.

Lo! in yon brilliant window-niche
    How statue-like I see thee stand,
The agate lamp within thy hand!
    Ah, Psyche, from the regions which
    Are Holy-Land!

Nicaean–*from the ancient Byzantine city of Nicaea, now the Turkish city of Iznik*

wont–*used to or accustomed to*   hyacinth–*deep red*   naiad–*river spirit* Psyche–*in Greek mythology, the beautiful wife of the god Cupid*

163

A DREAM WITHIN A DREAM

In poetry, there are a few ideas we hear over and over again. It is as though certain thoughts live in the soul of every poet. This poem contains one of those ideas. In the second stanza, Poe tells us that the days of life slip through his fingers like grains of sand, and no matter how he tries, he cannot stop the passage of time. It is an idea that was repeated a hundred years later by another American, a man named Thornton Wilder, who wrote,"Do any human beings ever realize life while they live it? Every minute? No, the Saints and Poets, maybe they do some."

Take this kiss upon the brow!
And, in parting from you now,
This much let me avow—
You are not wrong, who deem
That my days have been a dream;
Yet if Hope has flown away
In a night, or in a day,
In a vision, or in none,
Is it therefore the less gone?
All that we see or seem
Is but a dream within a dream.

I stand amid the roar
Of a surf-tormented shore,
And I hold within my hand
Grains of the golden sand—
How few! yet how they creep
Through my fingers to the deep,
While I weep—while I weep!
O God! can I not grasp
Them with a tighter clasp?
O God! can I not save
One from the pitiless wave?
Is *all* that we see or seem
But a dream within a dream?

THE BELOVED PHYSICIAN

This is a small part of a poem that was originally nine stanzas long. These few lines are all that remain. We find them quoted in a letter written by Marie Louise Shew, the lady to whom the poem was written. It was she who eventually lost or perhaps destroyed the poem.

In her letter she says, "I came up a country doctor's only daughter, with a taste for painting and a heart for loving all the world. I saved Mr. Poe's life at this time...at best, when he was well Mr. Poe's pulse beat only ten regular beats, after which it suspended or intermitted." Ms. Shew took care of Poe and nursed him back to health, and we suspect that she is the "beloved physician" referred to in the title of the poem.

In this poem, Poe describes how his heart beats ten times and then skips a beat. Without the rest of the poem, it is hard to hear exactly what he is trying to say. Yet we are lucky to have these few beautiful lines. They whisper a sense of calm—rest at last for a troubled soul.

The pulse beats ten and intermits.
God nerve the soul that ne'er forgets
In calm or storm, by night or day,
Its steady toil, its loyalty.

***

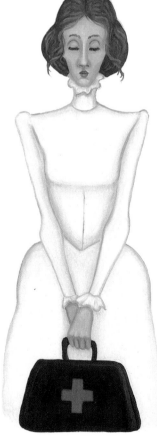

The pulse beats ten and intermits.
God shield the soul that ne'er forgets.

***

The pulse beats ten and intermits.
God guide the soul that ne'er forgets.

***

… so tired, so weary,
The soft head bows, the sweet eyes close;
The faithful heart yields to repose.

---

intermits–*stops for a moment*   repose–*rest*

THE BELLS

Two years before his death, Poe met the Reverend Cotesworth P. Bronson. Reverend Bronson was an elocutionist, someone who reads poetry out loud with a lot of expression. He encouraged Poe to write poems that could be performed aloud for an audience. Poe agreed to try, and "The Bells" was one of the poems that grew out of the reverend's suggestion. Be sure to read this poem out loud so you can hear how the sound and the meaning of the poem work together.

"The Bells" occurs in four parts, and each part has a different set of bells. In the first part we hear the tinkle of silver sleigh bells, and we think of the joy of childhood. When we hear the wedding bells of the second part, we think of love and hope. The bells of the third part are brazen alarm bells whose shriek is a warning of fire in the night. These bells make us think of the tragedies life can hold as we grow older. In the final part we hear iron bells. "Every sound that floats from the rust within their throats is a groan." What kind of bells do you think these are?

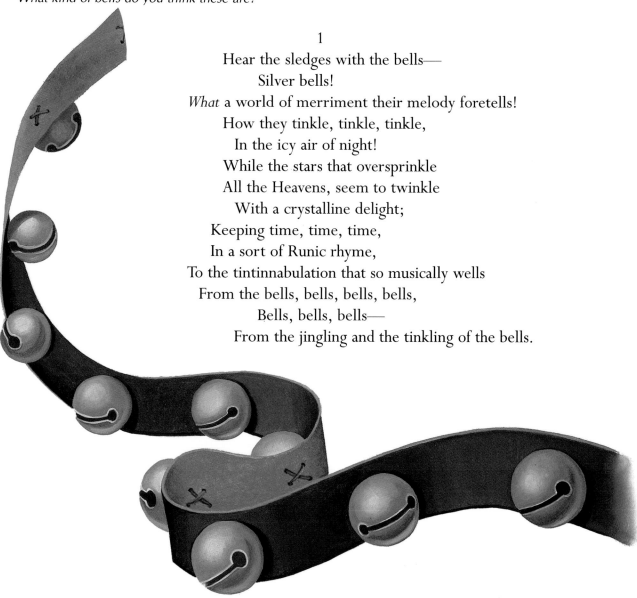

1

Hear the sledges with the bells—
Silver bells!
What a world of merriment their melody foretells!
How they tinkle, tinkle, tinkle,
In the icy air of night!
While the stars that oversprinkle
All the Heavens, seem to twinkle
With a crystalline delight;
Keeping time, time, time,
In a sort of Runic rhyme,
To the tintinnabulation that so musically wells
From the bells, bells, bells, bells,
Bells, bells, bells—
From the jingling and the tinkling of the bells.

---

sledges–*sleighs* crystalline–*clear crystal* runic–*ancient* tintinnabulation–*sound of a bell ringing*

2

Hear the mellow wedding bells—
Golden bells!
What a world of happiness their harmony foretells!
Through the balmy air of night
How they ring out their delight!—
From the molten-golden notes
And all in tune
What a liquid ditty floats
To the turtle-dove that listens while she gloats
On the moon!
Oh, from out the sounding cells
What a gush of euphony voluminously wells! How it swells!
How it swells!
How it dwells
On the future!—how it tells
Of the rapture that impels
To the swinging and the ringing
Of the bells, bells, bells!—
Of the bells, bells, bells, bells,
Bells, bells, bells—
To the rhyming and the chiming of the bells!

3

Hear the loud alarum bells—
Brazen bells!
What tale of terror, now, their turbulency tells!
In the startled ear of Night
How they scream out their affright!
Too much horrified to speak,
They can only shriek, shriek,
Out of tune,
In a clamorous appealing to the mercy of the fire—
In a mad expostulation with the deaf and frantic fire,
Leaping higher, higher, higher,

---

euphony–*pleasant sound*   voluminously–*largely*   rapture–*delightful feeling*

impels–*pushes onward*   alarum–*alarm*   brazen–*rudely bold*   turbulency–*violent movement*

affright–*fear*   expostulation–*attempt at persuading*

With a desperate desire
And a resolute endeavor
Now—now to sit, or never,
By the side of the pale-faced moon.
Oh, the bells, bells, bells!
What a tale their terror tells
Of despair!
How they clang and clash and roar!
What a horror they outpour
In the bosom of the palpitating air!
Yet the ear, it fully knows,
By the twanging
And the clanging,
How the danger ebbs and flows:—
Yes, the ear distinctly tells,
In the jangling
And the wrangling,
How the danger sinks and swells,
By the sinking or the swelling in the anger of the bells—
Of the bells—
Of the bells, bells, bells, bells,
Bells, bells, bells—
In the clamor and the clangor of the bells.

4

Hear the tolling of the bells—
Iron bells!
What a world of solemn thought their monody compels!
In the silence of the night
How we shiver with affright
At the melancholy meaning of the tone!
For every sound that floats
From the rust within their throats
Is a groan.
And the people—ah, the people

---

resolute–*determined* endeavor–*determined effort* palpitating–*throbbing*
monody–*death song* melancholy–*monotone*

They that dwell up in the steeple
　　All alone,
And who, tolling, tolling, tolling,
　　In that muffled monotone,
Feel a glory in so rolling
　　On the human heart a stone—
They are neither man nor woman—
They are neither brute nor human,
　　They are Ghouls:—
And their king it is who tolls:—
And he rolls, rolls, rolls, rolls
　　A Paean from the bells!
　　And his merry bosom swells
　　With the Paean of the bells!
　　And he dances and he yells;
Keeping time, time, time,
In a sort of Runic rhyme,
　　To the Paean of the bells—
　　Of the bells:—
　　Keeping time, time, time,
　　In a sort of Runic rhyme,
　　To the throbbing of the bells—
Of the bells, bells, bells—
　　To the sobbing of the bells:—
Keeping time, time, time,
　　As he knells, knells, knells,
In a happy Runic rhyme,
　　To the rolling of the bells—
Of the bells, bells, bells—
　　To the tolling of the bells—
Of the bells, bells, bells, bells,
　　Bells, bells, bells—
To the moaning and the groaning of the bells.

---

monotone–*single note*　ghouls–*evil graveyard spirits*　paean–*song of triumph*　knells–*rings*

ELDORADO

In this poem a knight goes in search of Eldorado, the mythical city of gold. He never finds it, and as he is about to die, he asks another wandering spirit where the city can be found. The last stanza is the spirit's reply. There may be times, as you grow older, when these lines will ring true in your ears.

Gaily bedight,
A gallant knight,
In sunshine and in shadow,
Had journeyed long
Singing a song,
In search of Eldorado.

But he grew old—
This knight so bold—
And o'er his heart a shadow
Fell as he found
No spot of ground
That looked like Eldorado.

And, as his strength
Failed him at length,
He met a pilgrim shadow—
"Shadow," said he,
"Where can it be—
This land of Eldorado?"

"Over the Mountains
Of the Moon,
Down the Valley of the Shadow,
Ride, boldly ride."
The shade replied,—
"If you seek for Eldorado!"

---

bedight—*well-equipped*

ROMANCE

This poem was one of Poe's favorites. He used it once as a preface and again as an introduction to books of his poems. He particularly liked the first five lines of the second stanza. Be careful: "romance" as used here does not mean "love"; it means an extravagant story based on things that cannot be true.

In the first stanza, Poe tells us that, as a child, his life was like a beautiful parakeet ("paroquet"), full of colorful stories that encouraged him to read and become wise beyond his years. In the second stanza, he tells us that his life as a young man was like a condor, a bird of prey that has no time for beauty. Then Poe predicts that there will come a more peaceful time in his life, and promises us that when that time comes, his heart will sing again like strings of a musical instrument.

1

Romance who loves to nod and sing
With drowsy head and folded wing
Among the green leaves as they shake
Far down within some shadowy lake
To me a painted paroquet
Hath been—a most familiar bird—
Taught me my alphabet to say—
To lisp my very earliest word
While in the wild wood I did lie
A child—with a most knowing eye.

2

Of late, eternal Condor years
So shake the very air on high
With tumult, as they thunder by,
I hardly have had time for cares
Thro' gazing on th' unquiet sky!
And, when an hour with calmer wings
Its down upon my spirit flings—
That little time with lyre and rhyme
To while away—forbidden things!
My heart would feel to be a crime
Did it not tremble with the strings!

---

condor–*large vulture* tumult–*disturbance* lyre–*small harp*

FOR ANNIE

This poem was written to Nancy Richmond, whose nickname was Annie. She was Poe's friend but not his "girlfriend." In a letter to her, Poe wrote, "I am so ill...in body and mind, that I feel I cannot live, unless I can feel your sweet, gentle, loving hand pressed upon my forehead—oh my pure, virtuous, generous, beautiful, beautiful sister Annie!"

This tender poem is about the healing power of her friendship. Poe is lying in bed. He has just overcome a "lingering illness" and he lies so still that you might think he is dead. But he is not dead; he is aglow "with the light of the love of my Annie." In this poem you can find the real Edgar Allan Poe.

Thank Heaven! the crisis—
   The danger is past,
And the lingering illness
   Is over at last—
And the fever called "Living"
   Is conquered at last.

Sadly, I know
   I am shorn of my strength,
And no muscle I move
   As I lie at full length—
But no matter!—I feel
   I am better at length.

And I rest so composedly
   Now, in my bed,
That any beholder
   Might fancy me dead—
Might start at beholding me,
   Thinking me dead.

The moaning and groaning,
   The sighing and sobbing,
Are quieted now,
   With that horrible throbbing
At heart:—ah that horrible,
   Horrible throbbing!

The sickness—the nausea—
   The pitiless pain—
Have ceased, with the fever
   That maddened my brain—
With the fever called "Living"
   That burned in my brain.

And oh! of all tortures
   That torture the worst
Has abated—the terrible
   Torture of thirst
For the naphthalene river
   Of Passion accurst:—
I have drunk of a water
   That quenches all thirst:—

Of a water that flows,
   With a lullaby sound,
From a spring but a very few
   Feet under ground—
From a cavern not very far
   Down under ground.

---

shorn–*deprived* composedly–*calmly* abated–*stopped* naphthalene–*cleansing* accurst–*cursed*

And ah! let it never
　　Be foolishly said
That my room it is gloomy
　　And narrow my bed;
For man never slept
　　In a different bed—
And, to *sleep*, you must slumber
　　In just such a bed.

My tantalized spirit
　　Here blandly reposes,
Forgetting, or never
　　Regretting, its roses—
Its old agitations
　　Of myrtles and roses:

For now, while so quietly
　　Lying, it fancies
A holier odor
　　About it, of pansies—
A rosemary odor,
　　Commingled with pansies—
With rue and the beautiful
　　Puritan pansies.

And so it lies happily,
　　Bathing in many
A dream of the truth
　　And the beauty of Annie—
Drowned in a bath
　　Of the tresses of Annie.

She tenderly kissed me,
　　She fondly caressed,
And then I fell gently
　　To sleep on her breast—
Deeply to sleep
　　From the heaven of her breast.

When the light was extinguished,
　　She covered me warm,
And she prayed to the angels
　　To keep me from harm—
To the queen of the angels
　　To shield me from harm.

And I lie so composedly,
　　Now, in my bed,
(Knowing her love)
　　That you fancy me dead—
And I rest so contentedly,
　　Now, in my bed,
(With her love at my breast)
　　That you fancy me dead—
That you shudder to look at me,
　　Thinking me dead:—

But my heart it is brighter
　　Than all of the many
Stars of the sky,
　　For it sparkles with Annie—
It glows with the light
　　Of the love of my Annie—
With the thought of the light
　　Of the eyes of my Annie.

---

tantalized–*tormented*

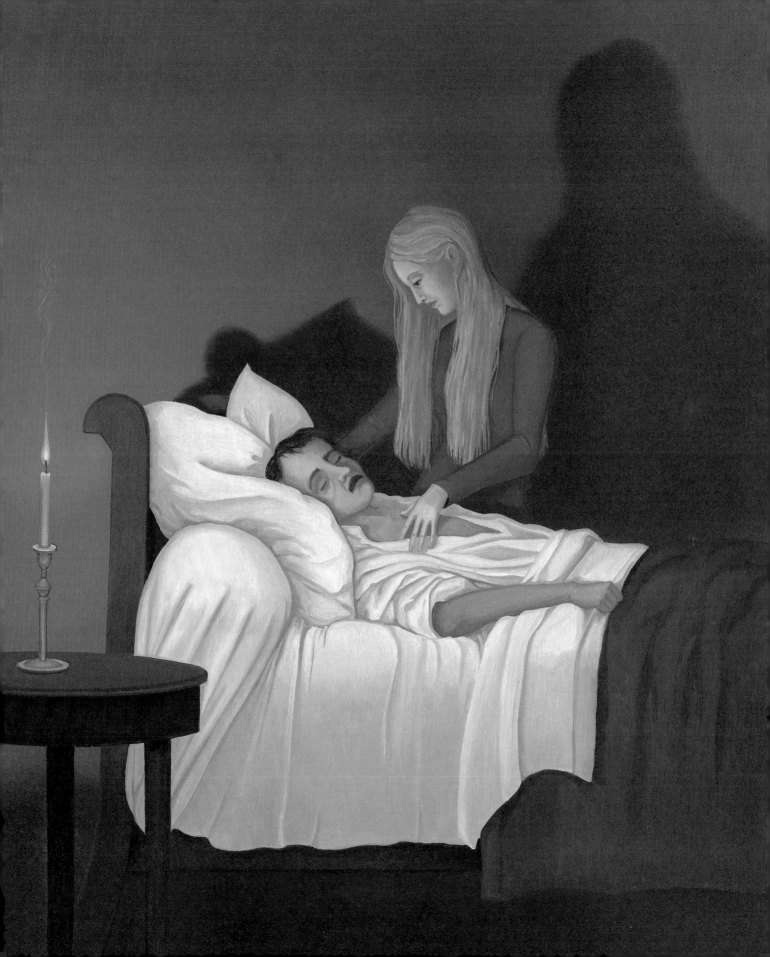

EULALIE—A SONG

This poem should encourage young poets. It proves that even a great poet can sometimes write a not-too-great poem. These verses are in the voice of a man very much in love with his wife. In the third to last line, "Astarté" refers to a heavenly body so bright that it shines even during daylight. This is probably the moon. Astarté, the mother goddess of Phoenicia, is often incorrectly believed to be a moon goddess.

I dwelt alone
In a world of moan,
And my soul was a stagnant tide,
Till the fair and gentle Eulalie became my blushing bride—
Till the yellow-haired young Eulalie became my smiling bride.

Ah, less—less bright
The stars of the night
Than the eyes of the radiant girl!
And never a flake
That the vapor can make
With the moon-tints of purple and pearl,
Can vie with the modest Eulalie's most unregarded curl—
Can compare with the bright-eyed Eulalie's most humble and careless curl.

Now Doubt—now Pain
Come never again,
For her soul gives me sigh for sigh,
And all day long
Shines, bright and strong,
Astarté within the sky,
While ever to her dear Eulalie upturns her matron eye—
While ever to her young Eulalie upturns her violet eye.

To _____ _____

Poe addresses this poem to an unnamed woman. He tells her that she is wonderful, so if she wants to be loved, she should simply be herself, and the world will take it as its "duty" to love her. This poem appears in several versions, each dedicated to a different lady. Perhaps Poe used this poem to meet girls. The text was never published, but appears in an undated but clearly authentic manuscript.

Thou wouldst be loved?—then let thy heart
From its present pathway part not!
Being everything which now thou art,
Be nothing which thou are not.
So, with the world, thy winning ways,
Thy truth, thy youth, thy beauty,
Shall be a daily theme of praise,
And love, no more than duty.

From "THE FALL OF THE HOUSE OF USHER"

The narrator of this story receives a letter from his boyhood friend, Roderick Usher. Roderick complains of a mysterious illness, so the narrator decides to visit him to see if he can help. In this passage we see for the first time the mysterious House of Usher. The house gives us a strange feeling and sets the stage for what is about to be a very strange story.

During the whole of a dull, dark, and soundless day
In the autumn of the year,
When clouds hung low in the heavens,
I had been passing on horseback through dreary country
And found myself,
As shades of evening drew,
Within view of the melancholy House of Usher.
With an utter depression of soul
I looked upon the house…
   The bleak walls,
   The vacant eye-like windows,
   A few white trunks of decayed trees.
There was an iciness, a sinking, a sickening of the heart,
An unredeemed dreariness of thought.
I paused to think
What was it that so unnerved me in the House of Usher?
It was a mystery all insoluble.

---

insoluble–*unable to be solved*

From "THE PIT AND THE PENDULUM"

This passage describes the moment at which a man is sentenced to death. Later in the story the man is tortured by a deadly sharp pendulum that swings, like the relentless arm of a giant clock, ever lower above his chest.

The sentence—the dread sentence of death—
Was the last which reached my ears.
I heard no more
Yet, for a while, I saw.
I saw the lips of black-robed judges,
Thin to grotesqueness,
Thin with the intensity of their firmness,
Of immovable resolution,
Of stern contempt of human torture.
I saw the decrees of Fate still issuing from those lips.
I saw them writhe with deadly locution.
I saw them fashion the syllables of my name
And I shuddered.
Then my vision fell upon the seven tall candles upon the table.
At first they seemed white slender angels who would save me,
But then the angel forms became spectres,
With heads of flame,
And I saw that from them there would be no help.
And then the figures of the judges vanished.
All swallowed up in a mad running descent…
Then silence,
And stillness,
And night were the universe.

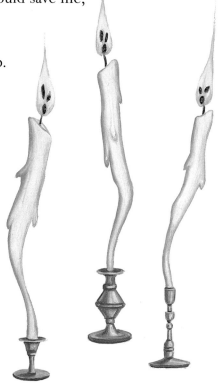

---

grotesqueness–*deformity* immovable–*unable to be moved* resolution–*determination*
writhe–*to twist in pain* locution–*speech* spectres–*ghosts*

From "THE MASQUE OF THE RED DEATH"

This is from a story about a prince who tries to hide from death in a walled castle. He is joined by a thousand of his friends. This passage describes how one night, at a masquerade party, a clock begins to chime. Later in the story, at the stroke of midnight, this same clock will announce the arrival of a strange and deadly visitor.

There stood against the western wall
A gigantic clock of ebony.
Its pendulum swung to and fro
With a dull, heavy, monotonous clang,
And when the minute-hand made the circuit of the face
And the hour was to be stricken,
There came from the brazen lungs of the clock
A sound which was clear and loud and deep
And exceedingly musical,
But of so peculiar a note
That the musicians of the orchestra were constrained to pause
And the waltzers ceased their evolutions,
And there was a brief disconcert of the whole gay company,
And the giddiest grew pale.
But when the echoes had fully ceased,
A light laughter at once pervaded the assembly,
The musicians looked at each other and smiled
And made whispering vows
That the next chiming of the clock should produce no similar emotion;
And then,
After the lapse of sixty minutes,
There came yet another chiming of the clock,
And the same disconcert and meditation as before.

---

constrained–*forced* evolutions–*twirling movements* disconcert–*worried disturbance*

From "THE TELL-TALE HEART"

"The Tell-Tale Heart" is a story about an insane murderer. This passage describes how he prepares to commit his ghastly crime.

You fancy me mad.
Madmen know nothing.
But you should have seen *me*.
You should have seen how wisely I proceeded,
With what caution,
With what foresight.
Every night, about midnight,
I turned the latch of his door
And opened it—oh, so gently!
And then,
When I had made an opening sufficient for my head,
I put in a dark lantern,
All closed so that no light shone out,
And then I thrust in my head.
How cunningly I thrust it in!
I moved it slowly—very, very slowly,
So that I might not disturb the old man's sleep.
It took me an hour.
Ha! Would a mad man have been so wise as this?
And then
I undid it just so much that a single thin ray fell upon the vulture eye.
This I did for seven long nights,
Every night just at midnight,
But I found the eye always closed;
And so it was impossible to do the work
For it was not the old man who vexed me,
But his evil eye.

From "THE BLACK CAT"

In this story, a condemned criminal tells how the howl of a black cat led police to discover the body of his victim.

I rapped heavily, with a cane
Upon that very portion of the brick-work,
But…
No sooner had the reverberation of my blows sunk into silence
I was answered by a voice from within the tomb,
By a cry,
At first muffled and broken, like the sobbing of a child,
And then quickly swelling into one long, loud, and continuous scream,
Utterly inhuman…
A howl…
A wailing shriek…
Half of horror and half of triumph
Such as might have arisen out of hell
From the throats of the damned in their agony
And the demons that exult in the damnation.

---

reverberation–*echo*   exult–*triumph*

From "THE CASK OF AMONTILLADO"

With the promise of Amontillado wine, the villain of this story leads his victim to a dead end deep in the underground passages of his family tomb. What happens next is perhaps one of the most haunting crimes in the body of English literature.

We continued in search of the Amontillado.
We passed through low arches
And descending again,
Arrived at a deep crypt
In which the foulness of the air
Caused our flambeaux rather to glow than flame.
At the most remote end of the crypt
There appeared another...less spacious.
Its walls had been lined with human bones
Piled to the vault overhead in the fashion of the catacombs.
Within the wall we perceived a still interior recess,
In depth about four feet,
In width three,
In height six or seven.
It seemed to have been constructed for no especial use,
The interval between two colossal supports of the roof,
And backed by one circumscribing wall of solid granite.
He stepped unsteadily forward,
While I followed immediately at his heels.
In an instant he had reached the extremity of the niche,
And finding his progress arrested by the rock,
Stood stupidly bewildered.
A moment more and I had fettered him to the granite.
"The Amontillado!" ejaculated my friend.

---

crypt–*underground passage*   flambeaux–*torches*   catacombs–*underground cemetery with spaces for corpses*
colossal–*giant*   circumscribing–*enclosing*   niche–*hollow place in a wall*
fettered–*bound with chains*   ejaculated–*spoke out suddenly*

From "HOP-FROG"

This story is about a king who has a court jester, a dwarf named Hop-Frog. The king forces the jester to drink wine, even though he knows it will make him crazy and sick. In the end the jester destroys the king. When we read this story, it's easy to believe that Poe knew his alcohol addiction was bad for him and that he wished, like little Hop-Frog, that he could get rid of it.

"Come here, Hop-Frog," said the king,
"Swallow this
And then let us have the benefit of your invention.
We want characters—
Characters, man, something novel.
We are wearied with this everlasting sameness.
Come drink!
The wine will brighten your wits."
The command to drink forced the tears to Hop-Frog's eyes,
Bitter drops fell into the goblet as he took it,
Humbly,
From the hand of the tyrant.
"Ha! Ha! Ha!" roared the king,
As the dwarf reluctantly drained the beaker.
Poor fellow!
Hop-Frog's large eyes gleamed…
He placed the goblet nervously on the table,
And looked round upon the company with a half-insane stare.

From "THE PREMATURE BURIAL"

This is a bright spot from an otherwise very dark story about a man who lives with a fear of being buried alive. Unlike most of Poe's characters, he avoids the unhappy ending.

Out of evil proceeded good—
  My soul acquired tone,
  I went abroad,
  I took vigorous exercise,
  I breathed the free air of Heaven,
  I thought upon other subjects than Death,
  And I read no bugaboo tales—such as this.
In short I became a new man,
And lived life.

bugaboo–*ghost*

Walt Whitman

Edited by Jonathan Levin
Illustrated by Jim Burke

WALT WHITMAN: I TRAMP A PERPETUAL JOURNEY

When Walt Whitman began publishing his poems in the mid-1800s, he forever changed people's sense of what a poet could be, and what a poem could look and sound like.

For Whitman, poetry was no schoolroom or parlor exercise. It wasn't an "indoor" activity at all. Instead, poetry had to breathe the open air. It had to start in the earth, just as a tree sets its roots deep in the soil, and then take flight, just as the tree shoots its branches into the sky.

Whitman liked to think of the poet as a kind of tramp: someone who travelled far and wide, meeting new people along the way, constantly seeking out new experiences and new encounters. He also liked to think of himself as the poet of the common man and woman. He admired people who worked hard, especially people who worked with their hands, and he often even made them the subject of his poems. More than anything else, though, he loved the diversity of life: so many different people, so many different kinds of plants and animals, cities and farms, dreams and visions. As a kind of poetic tramp, Whitman set out to encounter all this variety of life and to make it all hang together in his poems. Nobody had ever before tried to put so much into a poem.

Take a quick look at any poem in this book—just look at it, without even reading it. Whitman's lines almost seem to run right off the page. Before Whitman, the true mark of a poem was its regular pattern of meter and rhyme: the poet sought to shape his emotions and ideas into an organized form. Whitman's long lines are not usually structured in this way. In fact, they often seem to flow across the page in what looks like an uncontrollable flood of words. This happens because he is always trying to get so much of the detail of his world into his poems.

Read these poems aloud. Try to catch the sound of Whitman's voice in them. Whitman is said to have recited poetry aloud as he walked along the Long Island sea shore, and you can sometimes almost hear the rhythm of the surf in his poems. You can also sometimes hear the voice of a prophet, as when he cries out, "Unscrew the locks from the doors! Unscrew the doors themselves from the jambs!" Whitman loved the sound of the human voice, in speech and in song, and always imagined himself "singing" aloud in his poems.

Walt Whitman was born at West Hills, Long Island, in New York on May 31, 1819. His father, Walter Whitman, was a carpenter and a house builder, and a staunch supporter of the ideals of the American Revolution. Walt attributed his creativity to the influence of his mother, Louisa Van Velsor Whitman. Walt eventually had seven brothers and sisters, of which he was the second oldest. When Walt was not quite four years old, the Whitmans moved to Brooklyn, New York, where Walt's father continued to build and sell houses. It was a difficult time economically, and Whitman's father suffered many losses selling the houses he built. Walt managed to attend public schools for six years, until the age of eleven, but was forced to go to work as an office boy to earn money for the family after that. This was all the formal education he ever received.

When Walt was six, the Marquis de Lafayette, one of the last surviving heroes from the Revolutionary War, visited Brooklyn for a Fourth of July celebration. According to a story Whitman often told, General Lafayette lifted a number of schoolchildren, including young Walt. In some versions of the story, General Lafayette even embraced the future poet before putting him down. Whitman liked to tell this story, probably because he viewed it as a passing of the torch of freedom from one generation to the next.

At the age of eleven, Whitman went to work at the law offices of James B. Clarke and his son, Edward Clarke. Besides helping Walt with his handwriting and composition, Edward Clarke also signed Walt up with the local lending library, which marks the beginning of Walt's lifelong love of literature. Among his earliest favorites were the *Arabian Nights*, the historical novels and poems of Sir Walter Scott, and the adventure novels of another ground-breaking American writer, James Fenimore Cooper.

After working in law offices and a physician's office, Walt went to work for a newspaper. He began as an apprentice compositor, setting type for various local newspapers. Eventually, beginning in his mid-teens, he also began writing short pieces that appeared in the papers. Like many well-known authors, Whitman began his literary career as a journalist, reporting on a wide variety of topics. He was often asked to review books, operas, and plays during these years, a task that allowed him to indulge in his favorite pastimes: reading and attending the theater, especially opera.

With the continued problems of the real-estate market, Walter Whitman, Sr. moved his family back to Long Island. Walt, still a teenager, stayed behind in Brooklyn to continue working at various newspapers. Eventually, however, he rejoined his family and became a schoolteacher on Long Island. From his late teens into his twenties, Whitman alternated working as a teacher and as a compositor/journalist, depending on the kind of work he could find. Whitman was not your average mid-nineteenth-century schoolteacher. For one thing, he refused to hit his students, which made many local residents suspicious of his "lax" methods as a teacher!

By 1841, Whitman was back again in New York City, working as a compositor and writing stories for the papers. It was at this time that he was assigned to cover the New York City lectures of a visiting New England speaker already famous throughout the country, Ralph Waldo Emerson. Emerson would have a tremendous impact on Whitman's sense of what he could do as a writer. Emerson encouraged his audience to follow their inner promptings in all things. In one of the talks Whitman heard, Emerson called for a new kind of poet, one who would set free the imagination and, by doing so, transform the world.

Whitman worked at many different papers during this period, finding himself forced out of one job because he supported the principle that slavery be prohibited in all newly annexed territories—the very issue that eventually led to the Civil War. Whitman did a brief stint at a New Orleans paper, a period most notable for Whitman's journey to and from New Orleans. He travelled by train to Cumberland, then by horse-drawn stage to Wheeling, West Virginia, where he caught the steamboat that sailed the Ohio and Mississippi Rivers to New Orleans; he returned a little over two months later by steamboat up the Mississippi and across the Great Lakes, where, after taking the train to Niagara and Albany, he caught another steamboat that took him down the Hudson River to Manhattan. Whitman's fascination with American places was energized by these trips.

When his family returned to Brooklyn, Whitman again lived with them, travelling almost daily by ferry to Manhattan. This was the period during which he began to work on his first collection of poems, *Leaves of Grass*, which appeared when Whitman was 36 years old, in 1855. Whitman even assisted in typesetting the volume. The picture that appears in this book on page four, taken from the 1855 collection, depicts Whitman as the working-class man that he took such pride in being, dressed in a work shirt with the collar open, the tilt of his hat indicating his casual and even slightly mischievous air.

Early responses to Whitman's first book were often very critical. The *Boston Intelligencer* printed a scathing review, stating that Whiman "must be some escaped lunatic, raving in pitiable delirium." This was not an uncommon attitude at the time. Whitman was writing an entirely new kind of poetry. Who had ever seen poems about runaway slaves or about the miracles of everyday life, or a poem that began so boldly as "I celebrate myself"? Many readers disapproved of Whitman's subject matter and his style, neither of which seemed to them "refined" or "lofty" enough.

But Whitman also had his supporters. One of them was none other than Ralph Waldo Emerson, who had done so much to inspire Whitman in the first place. Emerson wrote Whitman a letter calling the book "the most extraordinary piece of wit and wisdom that America has yet contributed." "I greet you at the beginning of a great career," Emerson wrote, perhaps recognizing in Whitman the very poet he had called for in his lecture "The Poet."

Whitman was so fond of this letter that he had it reprinted in the second edition of his *Leaves of Grass*. Unfortunately, he never asked Emerson's permission, which upset Emerson, since it had in fact been written in personal correspondence. The two never managed to develop much of a friendship after that, and Emerson eventually even joked that Whitman was "half song-thrush, half alligator."

Whitman's father died on July 11, 1855, just days after *Leaves of Grass* appeared, leaving Walt to provide for his mother and siblings. Whitman would suffer financial difficulties for much of the rest of his life. He borrowed money and worked when he could as a newspaper editor. In 1860, a Boston publisher offered to print a third edition of *Leaves of Grass*. Whitman earned an impressive $1,000 from this edition, but the publishers went bankrupt shortly after publishing the book, and once again Whitman was strapped for money.

Over the years, Whitman published several editions of *Leaves of Grass*, revising old poems and adding new ones to the constantly growing collection. In all, Whitman published nine editions of *Leaves of Grass* in his lifetime.

Soon after Whitman prepared the 1860 edition, his brother George was wounded fighting in the battle of Fredericksburg in the Civil War. Whitman went to Washington, D.C. to be with George, who was recovering in a field hospital from a wound to the cheek. In Washington, Whitman was drawn into the orbit of the war, not as a soldier, but as a volunteer nurse. He worked as a clerk at a government office in the morning and visited the wounded in the Washington hospitals in the afternoon. He assisted these soldiers in any way he could, bringing them small gifts, talking with them, and occasionally writing out letters to family members that the soldiers would dictate to him (much like the letter in "Come Down from the Fields Father," page 31).

The Civil War (1861-1865) proved to be a crucial period in Whitman's life. Long a vocal opponent of slavery, he was also, like Abraham Lincoln, a determined supporter of the Union. Lincoln became another great hero to Whitman. Stories about Lincoln's own admiration of Whitman have also been told, but these probably have more legend in them than truth. Whitman himself claimed that he and Lincoln would regularly "exchange bows, and very cordial ones." In any event, Whitman admired Lincoln's force of character and his effort to bring an end to slavery and preserve the Union. Devastated when the President was assassinated in 1865—Whitman called it the "crowning crime of the Rebellion"—he wrote some of his best poems to mourn the passing of Lincoln (see "O Captain! My Captain!" and "When Lilacs Last in the Dooryard Bloom'd," pages 38 and 40).

After working as an office clerk in Washington, D.C. for several years, Whitman suffered a stroke in 1873. He moved to Camden, New Jersey soon after the stroke, where his mother died within three days of his arrival. Whitman would spend the rest of his days, apart from occasional travel, in Camden, often receiving visitors, with whom he was always happy to pass an afternoon in conversation. He made an extraordinary impression on his visitors, confirming his informal title as "The Good Gray Poet."

Whitman never married and is generally believed never to have had any children. By the time he died in 1892, he was widely regarded as one of the most important and accomplished, and one of the best loved writers America had yet produced.

I Hear America Singing

Whitman printed this as one of several poems that introduce his Leaves of Grass. *Notice the diversity of voices that make up Whitman's image of "America Singing."*

I hear America singing, the varied carols I hear,
Those of mechanics, each one singing his as it should be blithe and strong,
The carpenter singing his as he measures his plank or beam,
The mason singing his as he makes ready for work, or leaves off work,
The boatman singing what belongs to him in his boat, the deckhand singing on the steamboat deck,
The shoemaker singing as he sits on his bench, the hatter singing as he stands,
The wood-cutter's song, the ploughboy's on his way in the morning, or at noon intermission or at sun-
　　down,
The delicious singing of the mother, or of the young wife at work, or of the girl sewing or washing,
Each singing what belongs to him or her and to none else,
The day what belongs to the day—at night the party of young fellows, robust, friendly,
Singing with open mouths their strong melodious songs.

blithe—*happy, carefree*　　　　　　　　　　　melodious—*musical*

On Land

O the gleesome saunter over fields and hillsides!
The leaves and flowers of the commonest weeds, the moist fresh stillness of the woods,
The exquisite smell of the earth at daybreak, and all through the forenoon.

—from "A Song of Joys"

MIRACLES

With a little imagination, you can always finds miracles in what seems most ordinary and plain. Whitman uses one of his favorite poetic devices here, the catalogue, to demonstrate just how many miracles we encounter every day.

Why, who makes much of a miracle?
As to me I know of nothing else but miracles,
Whether I walk the streets of Manhattan,
Or dart my sight over the roofs of houses toward the sky,
Or wade with naked feet along the beach just in the edge of the water,
Or stand under trees in the woods,
Or talk by day with any one I love, or sleep in the bed at night with any one I love,
Or sit at table at dinner with the rest,
Or look at strangers opposite me riding in the car,
Or watch honey-bees busy around the hive of a summer forenoon,
Or animals feeding in the fields,
Or birds, or the wonderfulness of insects in the air,
Or the wonderfulness of the sundown, or of stars shining so quiet and bright,
Or the exquisite delicate thin curve of the new moon in spring;
These with the rest, one and all, are to me miracles,
The whole referring, yet each distinct and in its place.

To me every hour of the light and dark is a miracle,
Every cubic inch of space is a miracle,
Every square yard of the surface of the earth is spread with the same,
Every foot of the interior swarms with the same.

To me the sea is a continual miracle,
The fishes that swim—the rocks—the motion of the waves—the ships with men in them,
What stranger miracles are there?

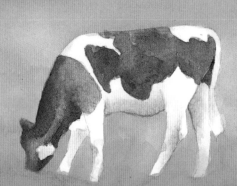

SONG OF MYSELF

"Song of Myself" is the first poem of Whitman's first book. It is made up of 52 sections, of which the first, sixth, and ninth are given here. These sections use the image of the grass and hay as symbol for the never-ending processes of life and death.

I celebrate myself, and sing myself,
And what I assume you shall assume,
For every atom belonging to me as good belongs to you.

I loafe and invite my soul,
I lean and loafe at my ease observing a spear of summer grass.

❖ ❖ ❖

A child said *What is the grass?* fetching it to me with full hands;
How could I answer the child? I do not know what it is any more than he.
I guess it must be the flag of my disposition, out of hopeful green stuff woven.

Or I guess it is the handkerchief of the Lord,
A scented gift and remembrancer designedly dropt,
Bearing the owner's name someway in the corners, that we
        may see and remark, and say *Whose?*

Or I guess the grass is itself a child, the produced babe of the vegetation.

Or I guess it is a uniform hieroglyphic,
And it means, Sprouting alike in broad zones and narrow zones,
Growing among black folks as among white,
Kanuck, Tuckahoe, Congressman, Cuff, I give them the same,
        I receive them the same.

And now it seems to me the beautiful uncut hair of graves.

Tenderly will I use you curling grass,
It may be you transpire from the breasts of young men,
It may be if I had known them I would have loved them,
It may be you are from old people, or from offspring taken soon out of their mothers' laps,
And here you are the mothers' laps.

This grass is very dark to be from the white heads of old mothers,
Darker than the colorless beards of old men,
Dark to come from under the faint red roofs of mouths.

202

O I perceive after all so many uttering tongues,
And I perceive they do not come from the roofs of mouths for nothing.

I wish I could translate the hints about the dead young men and women,
And the hints about old men and mothers, and the offspring taken soon out of their laps.

What do you think has become of the young and old men?
And what do you think has become of the women and children?

They are alive and well somewhere,
The smallest sprout shows there is really no death,
And if ever there was it led forward life, and does not wait at the end to arrest it,
And ceas'd the moment life appear'd.

All goes onward and outward, nothing collapses,
And to die is different from what any one supposed, and luckier.

The big doors of the country barn stand open and ready,
The dried grass of the harvest-time loads the slow-drawn wagon,
The clear light plays on the brown gray and green intertinged,
The armfuls are pack'd to the sagging mow.

I am there, I help, I came stretch'd atop of the load,
I felt its soft jolts, one leg reclined on the other,
I jump from the cross-beams and seize the clover and timothy,
And roll head over heels and tangle my hair full of wisps.

hieroglyphic: *ancient Egyptian picture-writing system, difficult to decipher; a "uniform hieroglyphic" would refer to the same mystery in all places.*
Kanuck—*French Canadian*
Tuckahoe—*Tidewater Virginian (from "tuckahoe," an edible fungus native to Virginia)*

Cuff—*African American*
intertinged—*mixed*
transpire: *to come or grow*

SPARKLES FROM THE WHEEL

A crowd of children gathers around a knife-grinder who has set up the tools of his trade on a city streetcorner. The "sparkles from the wheel" are caused by the knife as it is sharpened against the turning grindstone.

Where the city's ceaseless crowd moves on the livelong day,
Withdrawn I join a group of children watching, I pause aside with them.

By the curb toward the edge of the flagging,
A knife-grinder works at his wheel sharpening a great knife,
Bending over he carefully holds it to the stone, by foot and knee,
With measur'd tread he turns rapidly, as he presses with light but firm hand,
Forth issue then in copious golden jets,
Sparkles from the wheel.

The scene and all its belongings, how they seize and affect me,
The sad sharp-chinn'd old man with worn clothes and broad shoulder-band of leather,
Myself effusing and fluid, a phantom curiously floating, now here absorb'd and arrested,
The group, (an unminded point set in a vast surrounding,)
The attentive, quiet children, the loud, proud, restive base of the streets,
The low hoarse purr of the whirling stone, the light-press'd blade,
Diffusing, dropping, sideways-darting, in tiny showers of gold,
Sparkles from the wheel.

flagging—*the pavement*　　　　　　restive—*restless*
copious—*plentiful*　　　　　　　　diffusing—*spreading out*
effusing—*overflowing*

TO A LOCOMOTIVE IN WINTER

This and the next poem are presented as recitatives, or formal oral presentations, usually made before an audience. Whitman's description captures the force and beauty of the train, almost as if it were a living creature. Indeed, the train almost seems to come to life in the poem.

Thee for my recitative,
Thee in the driving storm even as now, the snow, the winter-day declining,
Thee in thy panoply, thy measur'd dual throbbing and thy beat convulsive,
Thy black cylindric body, golden brass and silvery steel,
Thy ponderous side-bars, parallel and connecting rods, gyrating, shuttling at thy sides,
Thy metrical, now swelling pant and roar, now tapering in the distance,
Thy great protruding head-light fix'd in front,
Thy long, pale, floating vapor-pennants, tinged with delicate purple,
The dense and murky clouds out-belching from thy smoke-stack,
Thy knitted frame, thy springs and valves, the tremulous twinkle of thy wheels,
Thy train of cars behind, obedient, merrily following,
Through gale or calm, now swift, now slack, yet steadily careering;
Type of the modern—emblem of motion and power—pulse of the continent,
For once come serve the Muse and merge in verse, even as here I see thee,
With storm and buffeting gusts of wind and falling snow,
By day thy warning ringing bell to sound its notes,
By night thy silent signal lamps to swing.

Fierce-throated beauty!
Roll through my chant with all thy lawless music, thy swinging lamps at night,
Thy madly-whistled laughter, echoing, rumbling like an earth-quake, rousing all,
Law of thyself complete, thine own track firmly holding,
(No sweetness debonair of tearful harp or glib piano thine,)
Thy trills of shrieks by rocks and hills return'd,
Launch'd o'er the prairies wide, across the lakes,
To the free skies unpent and glad and strong.

panoply—*magnificent attire*　　　　vapor-pennants—*trailing smoke*
ponderous—*heavy*　　　　　　　　careering—*rushing forward*
gyrating—*turning*　　　　　　　　debonair—*charming*
metrical—*rhythmic*

THE OX-TAMER

Before there were tractors, farmers used oxen to pull their ploughs. These oxen had to be trained. Whitman expresses his admiration for the ox-tamer's abilities, and manages to put in a few words for the great beauty of the oxen themselves.

In a far-away northern county in the placid pastoral region,
Lives my farmer friend, the theme of my recitative, a famous tamer of oxen,
There they bring him the three-year-olds and the four-year-olds to break them,
He will take the wildest steer in the world and break him and tame him,
He will go fearless without any whip where the young bullock chafes up and down the yard,
The bullock's head tosses restless high in the air with raging eyes,
Yet see you! how soon his rage subsides—how soon this tamer tames him;
See you! on the farms hereabout a hundred oxen young and old, and he is the man who has tamed them,
They all know him, all are affectionate to him;
See you! some are such beautiful animals, so lofty looking;
Some are buff-color'd, some mottled, one has a white line running along his back, some are brindled,
Some have wide flaring horns (a good sign)—see you! the bright hides,
See, the two with stars on their foreheads—see, the round bodies and broad backs,
How straight and square they stand on their legs—what fine sagacious eyes!
How they watch their tamer—they wish him near them—how they turn to look after him!
What yearning expression! how uneasy they are when he moves away from them;
Now I marvel what it can be he appears to them, (books, politics, poems, depart—all else departs,)
I confess I envy only his fascination—my silent, illiterate friend,
Whom a hundred oxen love there in his life on farms,
In the northern county far, in the placid pastoral region.

placid—*quiet, tranquil*   mottled—*spotted*
pastoral—*rural*   brindled—*streaked*
break—*to tame or train*   sagacious—*wise*
chafes—*moves restlessly*

209

A Man's Body at Auction

This poem is part of the longer poem "I Sing the Body Electric," in which Whitman celebrates the human body as an extension of the soul. Here, the speaker describes a slave who is being sold by an auctioneer, a common practice in the South before the Civil War.

A man's body at auction,
(For before the war I often go to the slave-mart and watch the sale,)
I help the auctioneer, the sloven does not half know his business.

Gentlemen look on this wonder,
Whatever the bids of the bidders they cannot be high enough for it,
For it the globe lay preparing quintillions of years without one animal or plant,
For it the revolving cycles truly and steadily roll'd.

In this head the all-baffling brain,
In it and below it the makings of heroes.

Examine these limbs, red, black, or white, they are cunning in tendon and nerve,
They shall be stript that you may see them.

Exquisite senses, life-lit eyes, pluck, volition,
Flakes of breast-muscle, pliant backbone and neck, flesh not flabby, good-sized arms and legs,
And wonders within there yet.

Within there runs blood,
The same old blood! the same red-running blood!
There swells and jets a heart, there all passions, desires, reachings, aspirations,
(Do you think they are not there because they are not express'd in parlors and lecture-rooms?)

This is not only one man, this the father of those who shall be fathers in their turns,
In him the start of populous states and rich republics,
Of him countless immortal lives with countless embodiments and enjoyments.

How do you know who shall come from the offspring of his offspring through the centuries?
(Who might you find you have come from yourself, if you could trace back through the centuries?)

sloven—*an uncultivated person*   volition—*will*
pluck—*courage*

I Think I Could Turn and Live with Animals

Whitman expresses not just his deep love of animals, but also his strong feeling of affinity with them. This poem comes from "Song of Myself."

I think I could turn and live with animals, they are so placid and self-
      contain'd,
I stand and look at them long and long.

They do not sweat and whine about their condition,
They do not lie awake in the dark and weep for their sins,
They do not make me sick discussing their duty to God,
Not one is dissatisfied, not one is demented with the mania of owning things,
Not one kneels to another, nor to his kind that lived thousands of years ago,
Not one is respectable or unhappy over the whole earth.

So they show their relations to me and I accept them,
They bring me tokens of myself, they evince them plainly in their possession.

I wonder where they get those tokens,
Did I pass that way huge times ago and negligently drop them?

Myself moving forward then and now and forever,
Gathering and showing more always and with velocity,
Infinite and omnigenous, and the like of these among them,
Not too exclusive toward the reachers of my remembrancers,
Picking out here one that I love, and now go with him on brotherly terms.

A gigantic beauty of a stallion, fresh and responsive to my caresses,
Head high in the forehead, wide between the ears,
Limbs glossy and supple, tail dusting the ground,
Eyes full of sparkling wickedness, ears finely cut, flexibly moving.

His nostrils dilate as my heels embrace him,
His well-built limbs tremble with pleasure as we race around and return.

I but use you a minute, then I resign you, stallion,
Why do I need your paces when I myself out-gallop them?
Even as I stand or sit passing faster than you.

tokens—*signs, small parts*   omnigenous—*belonging to all types and species*

At Sea

The untold want by life and land ne'er granted,
Now voyager sail thou forth to seek and find.
> —"The Untold Want"

ABOARD AT A SHIP'S HELM

Whitman compares the dangerous course of a ship's voyage with the path taken by the immortal soul. The sea is full of hidden dangers for the ship, but a ringing bell at least provides warning. What of the human soul's voyaging?

Aboard at a ship's helm,
A young steersman steering with care.

Through fog on a sea-coast dolefully ringing,
An ocean-bell—O a warning bell, rock'd by the waves.

O you give good notice indeed, you bell by the sea-reefs ringing,
Ringing, ringing, to warn the ship from its wreck-place.

For as on the alert O steersman, you mind the loud admonition,
The bows turn, the freighted ship tacking speeds away under her gray sails,
The beautiful and noble ship with all her precious wealth speeds away gayly and safe.

But O the ship, the immortal ship! O ship aboard the ship!
Ship of the body, ship of the soul, voyaging, voyaging, voyaging.

helm—*ship's steering mechanism*
dolefully—*cheerlessly, sadly*
admonition—*warning*
freighted—*full of freight*

214

THE WORLD BELOW THE BRINE

In describing the world beneath the surface of the sea, Whitman again uses the catalogue, here to emphasize the great variety of life found deep in the sea. In the last two lines of this poem, he speculates about how our human life might appear to beings inhabiting "other spheres" of which we are unaware.

The world below the brine,
Forests at the bottom of the sea, the branches and leaves,
Sea-lettuce, vast lichens, strange flowers and seeds, the thick tangle, openings, and pink turf,
Different colors, pale gray and green, purple, white, and gold, the play of light through the water,
Dumb swimmers there among the rocks, coral, gluten, grass, rushes, and the aliment of the swimmers,
Sluggish existences grazing there suspended, or slowly crawling close to the bottom,
The sperm-whale at the surface blowing air and spray, or disporting with his flukes,
The leaden-eyed shark, the walrus, the turtle, the hairy sea-leopard, and the sting-ray,
Passions there, wars, pursuits, tribes, sight in those ocean-depths, breathing that thick-breathing air, as so
    many do,
The change thence to the sight here, and to the subtle air breathed by beings like us who walk this sphere,
The change onward from ours to that of beings who walk other spheres.

brine—*sea-water*
gluten—*glutenous or gummy substances*
aliment—*food*
disporting—*playing*
flukes—*a whale's tail*

215

ON THE BEACH AT NIGHT

As clouds darken the starry sky, the speaker consoles a child with a lesson in things eternal. The sea and sky often bring out the mystic in Whitman.

On the beach at night,
Stands a child with her father,
Watching the east, the autumn sky.

Up through the darkness,
While ravening clouds, the burial clouds, in black masses spreading,
Lower sullen and fast athwart and down the sky,
Amid a transparent clear belt of ether yet left in the east,
Ascends large and calm the lord-star Jupiter,
And nigh at hand, only a very little above,
Swim the delicate sisters the Pleiades.

From the beach the child holding the hand of her father,
Those burial-clouds that lower victorious soon to devour all,
Watching, silently weeps.

Weep not, child,
Weep not, my darling,
With these kisses let me remove your tears,
The ravening clouds shall not long be victorious,
They shall not long possess the sky, they devour the stars only in apparition,
Jupiter shall emerge, be patient, watch again another night, the Pleiades shall emerge,
They are immortal, all those stars both silvery and golden shall shine out again,
The great stars and the little ones shall shine out again, they endure,
The vast immortal suns and the long-enduring pensive moons shall again shine.

Then dearest child mournest thou only for Jupiter?
Considerest thou alone the burial of the stars?

Something there is,
(With my lips soothing thee, adding I whisper,
I give thee the first suggestion, the problem and indirection,)
Something there is more immortal even than the stars,
(Many the burials, many the days and nights, passing away,)
Something that shall endure longer even than lustrous Jupiter,
Longer than sun or any revolving satellite,
Or the radiant sisters the Pleiades.

ravening—*devouring*
athwart—*across*
Pleiades—*a constella-*
  tion named for the
  seven daughters of
  Atlas
pensive—*thoughtful,*
  dreamy

217

DID YOU READ IN THE SEABOOKS...

Taken from "Song of Myself," this poem tells the story of the thrilling revolutionary-war sea battle between the American Serapis *and the British* BonHomme Richard.

Did you read in the seabooks of the oldfashioned frigate-fight?
Did you learn who won by the light of the moon and stars?

Our foe was no skulk in his ship, I tell you,
His was the English pluck, and there is no tougher or truer, and never was, and never will be;
Along the lowered eve he came, horribly raking us.

We closed with him....the yards entangled....the cannon touched,
My captain lashed fast with his own hands.

We had received some eighteen-pound shots under the water,
On our lower-gun-deck two large pieces had burst at the first fire, killing all around and blowing up overhead.

Ten o'clock at night, and the full moon shining and the leaks on the gain, and five feet of water reported,
The master-at-arms loosing the prisoners confined in the after-hold to give them a chance for themselves.

The transit to and from the magazine was now stopped by the sentinels,
They saw so many strange faces they did not know whom to trust.

Our frigate was afire....the other asked if we demanded quarters? if our colors were struck and the fighting done?

I laughed content when I heard the voice of my little captain,
We have not struck, he composedly cried, We have just begun our part of the fighting.

Only three guns were in use,
One was directed by the captain himself against the enemy's mainmast,
Two well-served with grape and canister silenced his musketry and cleared his decks.

The tops alone seconded the fire of this little battery, especially the maintop,
They all held out bravely during the whole of the action.

Not a moment's cease,
The leaks gained fast on the pumps....the fire eat toward the powder-magazine,
One of the pumps was shot away....it was generally thought we were sinking.

Serene stood the little captain,
He was not hurried....his voice was neither high nor low,
His eyes gave more light to us than our battle-lanterns.

Toward twelve at night, there in the beams of the moon they surrendered to us.

skulk—*coward*
yards—*poles that support the sails*
magazine—*munitions storehouse*
quarter—*merciful treatment in surrender*
struck—*lowered in surrender*
grape and canister—*cannonballs*

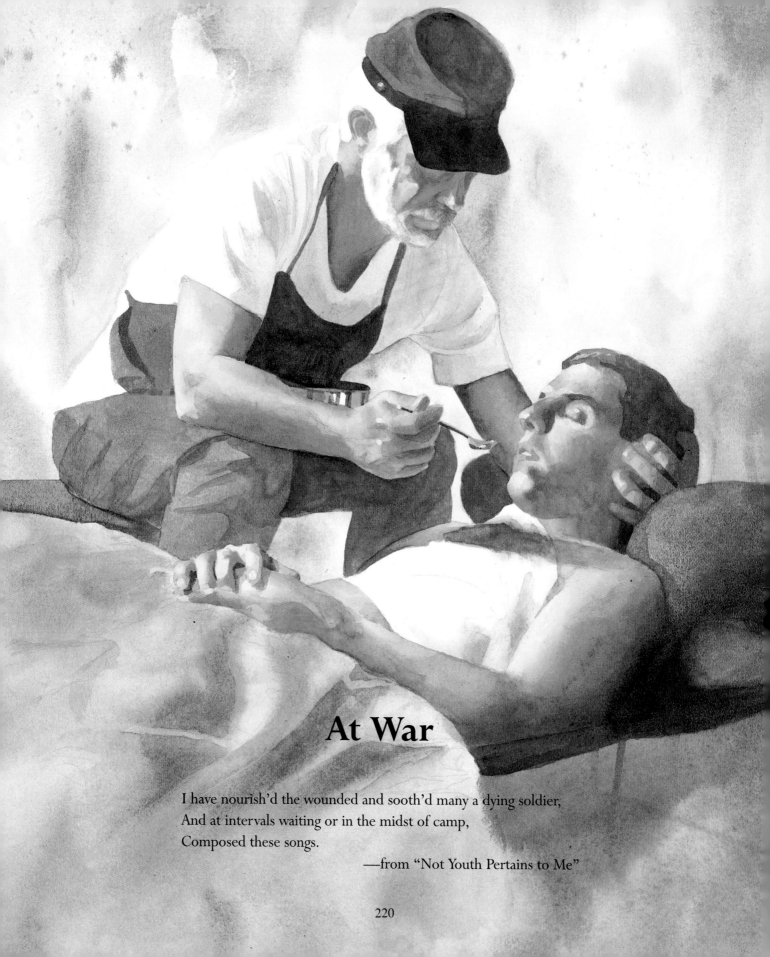

At War

I have nourish'd the wounded and sooth'd many a dying soldier,
And at intervals waiting or in the midst of camp,
Composed these songs.

—from "Not Youth Pertains to Me"

COME UP FROM THE FIELDS FATHER

This poem describes the war's devastation from the point of view of a family on a farm in Ohio. By the end of the poem, the focus is almost exclusively on the boy's mother, who must now come to terms with her grief.

Come up from the fields father, here's a letter from our Pete,
And come to the front door mother, here's a letter from thy dear son.

Lo, 'tis autumn,
Lo, where the trees, deeper green, yellower and redder,
Cool and sweeten Ohio's villages with leaves fluttering in the moderate wind,
Where apples ripe in the orchards hang and grapes on the trellis'd vines,
(Smell you the smell of the grapes on the vines?
Smell you the buckwheat where the bees were lately buzzing?)

Above all, lo, the sky so calm, so transparent after the rain, and with wondrous clouds,
Below too, all calm, all vital and beautiful, and the farm prospers well.

Down in the fields all prospers well,
But now from the fields come father, come at the daughter's call,
And come to the entry mother, to the front door come right away.

Fast as she can she hurries, something ominous, her steps trembling,
She does not tarry to smooth her hair nor adjust her cap.

Open the envelope quickly,
O this is not our son's writing, yet his name is sign'd,
O a strange hand writes for our dear son, O stricken mother's soul!
All swims before her eyes, flashes with black, she catches the main words only,
Sentences broken, *gunshot wound in the breast, cavalry skirmish, taken to hospital,*
At present low, but will soon be better.

Ah now the single figure to me,
Amid all teeming and wealthy Ohio with all its cities and farms,
Sickly white in the face and dull in the head, very faint,
By the jamb of a door leans.

Grieve not so, dear mother, (the just-grown daughter speaks through her sobs,
The little sisters huddle around speechless and dismay'd,)
See, dearest mother, the letter says Pete will soon be better.

Alas poor boy, he will never be better, (nor may-be needs to be better, that brave and simple soul,)
While they stand at home at the door he is dead already,
The only son is dead.

But the mother needs to be better,
She with thin form presently drest in black,
By day her meals untouch'd, then at night fitfully sleeping, often waking,
In the midnight waking, weeping, longing with one deep longing,
O that she might withdraw unnoticed, silent from life escape and withdraw,
To follow, to seek, to be with her dear dead son.

ominous—*vaguely frightening*

THE RUNAWAY SLAVE

The speaker here assists a runaway slave, defying federal laws that would have required him to turn the fugitive slave over to the authorities. This poem, taken from "Song of Myself," shows the kind, humanitarian spirit that escaped slaves sometimes encountered in the North.

The runaway slave came to my house and stopt outside,
I heard his motions crackling the twigs of the woodpile,
Through the swung half-door of the kitchen I saw him limpsy and weak,
And went where he sat on a log and led him in and assured him,
And brought water and fill'd a tub for his sweated body and bruis'd feet,
And gave him a room that enter'd from my own, and gave him some coarse clean clothes,
And remember perfectly well his revolving eyes and his awkwardness,
And remember putting plasters on the galls of his neck and ankles;
He staid with me a week before he was recuperated and pass'd north,
I had him sit next me at table, my fire-lock lean'd in the corner.

limpsy—*limp from weakness*   galls—*skin sores*
plasters—*medicated dressing for a wound*   fire-lock—*rifle*

THE ARTILLERYMAN'S VISION

Whitman wrote many poems about the Civil War, which he collected in a section of Leaves of Grass *called "Drum-Taps."*
The speaker in this poem has returned home, but continues to be haunted by powerful memories of the war.

While my wife at my side lies slumbering, and the wars are over long,
And my head on the pillow rests at home, and the vacant midnight passes,
And through the stillness, through the dark, I hear, just hear, the breath of my infant,
There in the room as I wake from sleep this vision presses upon me;
The engagement opens there and then in fantasy unreal,
The skirmishers begin, they crawl cautiously ahead, I hear the irregular snap! snap!
I hear the sounds of the different missiles, the short *t-h-t! t-h-t!* of the rifle-balls,
I see the shells exploding leaving small white clouds, I hear the great shells shrieking as they pass,
The grape like the hum and whirr of wind through the trees, (tumultuous now the contest rages,)
All the scenes at the batteries rise in detail before me again,
The crashing and smoking, the pride of the men in their pieces,
The chief-gunner ranges and sights his piece and selects a fuse of the right time,
After firing I see him lean aside and look eagerly off to note the effect;
Elsewhere I hear the cry of a regiment charging, (the young colonel leads himself this time with brandish'd
    sword,)
I see the gaps cut by the enemy's volleys, (quickly fill'd up, no delay,)
I breathe the suffocating smoke, then the flat clouds hover low concealing all;
Now a strange lull for a few seconds, not a shot fired on either side,
Then resumed the chaos louder than ever, with eager calls and orders of officers,
While from some distant part of the field the wind wafts to my ears a shout of applause, (some special suc-
    cess,)
And ever the sound of the cannon far or near, (rousing even in dreams a devilish exultation and all the old
    mad joy in the depths of my soul,)
And ever the hastening of infantry shifting positions, batteries, cavalry, moving hither and thither,
(The falling, dying, I heed not, the wounded dripping and red I heed not, some to the rear are hobbling,)
Grime, heat, rush, aide-de-camps galloping by or on a full run,
With the patter of small arms, the warning *s-s-t* of the rifles, (these in my vision I hear or see,)
And bombs bursting in air, and at night the vari-color'd rockets.

grape—*artillery*   fuse—*combustible cord used to light cannons*
batteries—*artillery unit*   volleys—*simultaneous gunfire*
pieces—*weapons*   aide-de-camps—*assistants to commanders*

O Captain! My Captain!

Although he is never mentioned by name, Abraham Lincoln is the subject of this and the following poem. Lincoln was assassinated on April 14, 1865, less than a week after the war had ended. This poem is one of Whitman's few poems written in meter and rhyme.

O Captain! my Captain! our fearful trip is done,
The ship has weather'd every rack, the prize we sought is won,
The port is near, the bells I hear, the people all exulting,
While follow eyes the steady keel, the vessel grim and daring;
   But O heart! heart! heart!
    O the bleeding drops of red,
     Where on the deck my Captain lies,
     Fallen cold and dead.

O Captain! my Captain! rise up and hear the bells;
Rise up—for you the flag is flung—for you the bugle trills,
For you bouquets and ribbon'd wreaths—for you the shores a-crowding,
For you they call, the swaying mass, their eager faces turning;
   Here Captain! dear father!
    This arm beneath your head!
    It is some dream that on the deck,
     You've fallen cold and dead.

My Captain does not answer, his lips are pale and still,
My father does not feel my arm, he has no pulse nor will,
The ship is anchor'd safe and sound, its voyage closed and done,
From fearful trip the victor ship comes in with object won;
   Exult O shores, and ring O bells!
    But I with mournful tread,
    Walk the deck my Captain lies,
     Fallen cold and dead.

WHEN LILACS LAST IN THE DOORYARD BLOOM'D

After his death, Lincoln's body was taken on a long procession from Washington, D.C. through several major American cities. The procession ended in Springfield, Illinois, where he was buried. It was spring, and lilacs, a common dooryard flower, were in bloom. The lilacs became Whitman's symbol for the mourning nation's enduring affection for Lincoln. These passages are drawn from a longer poem on Lincoln's death.

When lilacs last in the dooryard bloom'd,
And the great star early droop'd in the western sky in the night,
I mourn'd, and yet shall mourn with ever-returning spring.

Ever-returning spring, trinity sure to me you bring,
Lilac blooming perennial and drooping star in the west,
And thought of him I love.

❖ ❖ ❖

Coffin that passes through lanes and streets,
Through day and night with the great cloud darkening the land,
With the pomp of the inloop'd flags with the cities draped in black,
With the show of the States themselves as of crape-veil'd women standing,
With processions long and winding and the flambeaus of the night,
With the countless torches lit, with the silent sea of faces and the unbared heads,
With the waiting depot, the arriving coffin, and the sombre faces,
With dirges through the night, with the thousand voices rising strong and solemn,
With all the mournful voices of the dirges pour'd around the coffin,
The dim-lit churches and the shuddering organs—where amid these you journey,
With the tolling tolling bells' perpetual clang,
Here, coffin that slowly passes,
I give you my sprig of lilac.

dooryard—*area around the doorway to a house*
great star—*Venus, a symbol here for Lincoln*
inloop'd—*looped, or fastened, together*

flambeaus—*flaming torches*
sombre—*serious, gloomy*
dirges—*funeral songs*

Sky and Cosmos

After the dazzle of day is gone,
Only the dark, dark night shows to my eyes the stars;
After the clangor of organ majestic, or chorus, or perfect band,
Silent, athwart my soul, moves the symphony true.

— "After the Dazzle of Day"

A NOISELESS PATIENT SPIDER

Whitman develops an analogy between the spider, with its capacity to launch its web into the unknown, and the human soul. What kind of filaments does the human soul send forth?

A noiseless patient spider,
I mark'd where on a little promontory it stood isolated,
Mark'd how to explore the vacant vast surrounding,
It launch'd forth filament, filament, filament, out of itself,
Ever unreeling them, ever tirelessly speeding them.

And you O my soul where you stand,
Surrounded, detached, in measureless oceans of space,
Ceaselessly musing, venturing, throwing, seeking the spheres to connect them,
Till the bridge you will need be form'd, till the ductile anchor hold,
Till the gossamer thread you fling catch somewhere, O my soul.

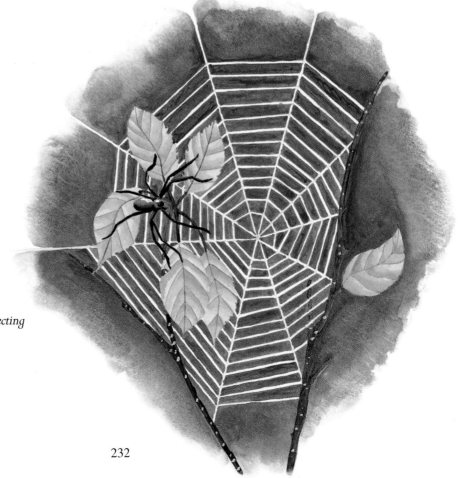

promontory—*a high point of land projecting
    over water or lower land*
filament—*a thread; the spider's web*
ductile—*easily shaped*
gossamer—*light and delicate*

THE DALLIANCE OF THE EAGLES

Whitman describes an encounter between two eagles, joined together,
high up in the sky, in a thrilling, playful, loving dance.

Skirting the river road, (my forenoon walk, my rest,)
Skyward in air a sudden muffled sound, the dalliance of the eagles,
The rushing amorous contact high in space together,
The clinching interlocking claws, a living, fierce, gyrating wheel,
Four beating wings, two beaks, a swirling mass tight grappling,
In tumbling turning clustering loops, straight downward falling,
Till o'er the river pois'd, the twain yet one, a moment's lull,
A motionless still balance in the air, then parting, talons loosing,
Upward again on slow-firm pinions slanting, their separate diverse flight,
She hers, he his, pursuing.

dalliance—*playful, sometimes romantic, activity*   talons—*claws*
amorous—*loving*   pinions—*wings*
gyrating—*revolving, turning*

WHEN I HEARD THE LEARN'D ASTRONOMER

Whitman juxtaposes the scientific lectures he attends on the subject of astronomy with his first-hand experience of the star-filled sky. He discovers something in the first-hand experience that the lectures cannot convey.

When I heard the learn'd astronomer,

When the proofs, the figures, were ranged in columns before me,

When I was shown the charts and diagrams, to add, divide, and measure them,

When I sitting heard the astronomer where he lectured with much applause in the lecture-room,

How soon unaccountable I became tired and sick,

Till rising and gliding out I wander'd off by myself,

In the mystical moist night-air, and from time to time,

Look'd up in perfect silence at the stars.

I TRAMP A PERPETUAL JOURNEY

This poem, taken from "Song of Myself," explores one of Whitman's favorite themes, the romance of travelling the open road. One of Whitman's key ideas here is that you must travel the road "for yourself."

I tramp a perpetual journey, (come listen all!)
My signs are a rain-proof coat, good shoes, and a staff cut from the woods,
No friend of mine takes his ease in my chair,
I have no chair, no church, no philosophy,
I lead no man to a dinner-table, library, exchange,
But each man and each woman of you I lead upon a knoll,
My left hand hooking you round the waist,
My right hand pointing to landscapes of continents and the public road.

Not I, not any one else can travel that road for you,
You must travel it for yourself.

It is not far, it is within reach,
Perhaps you have been on it since you were born and did not know,
Perhaps it is everywhere on water and on land.

Shoulder your duds dear son, and I will mine, and let us hasten forth,
Wonderful cities and free nations we shall fetch as we go.

If you tire, give me both burdens, and rest the chuff of your hand on my hip,
And in due time you shall repay the same service to me,
For after we start we never lie by again.

This day before dawn I ascended a hill and look'd at the crowded heaven,
And I said to my spirit *When we become the enfolders of those orbs, and the pleasure and knowledge of every thing in them, shall we be fill'd and satisfied then?*
And my spirit said, *No, we but level that lift to pass and continue beyond*.

duds—*clothes*   level that lift—*reach that height*
chuff—*probably the palm*

THE SPOTTED HAWK SWOOPS BY

The speaker compares himself to a hawk in this poem that concludes the long sequence "Song of Myself." Whitman takes leave of his reader, but promises to "return" in the form of the many reminders of the themes and images of his poems that the reader (you!) will encounter in the future.

The spotted hawk swoops by and accuses me, he complains of my gab and my loitering.

I too am not a bit tamed, I too am untranslatable,
I sound my barbaric yawp over the roofs of the world.

The last scud of day holds back for me,
It flings my likeness after the rest and true as any on the shadow'd wilds,
It coaxes me to the vapor and the dusk.

I depart as air, I shake my white locks at the runaway sun,
I effuse my flesh in eddies, and drift it in lacy jags.

I bequeath myself to the dirt to grow from the grass I love,
If you want me again look for me under your boot-soles.
You will hardly know who I am or what I mean,
But I shall be good health to you nevertheless,
And filter and fibre your blood.

Failing to fetch me at first keep encouraged,
Missing me one place search another,
I stop somewhere waiting for you.

gab—*pointless talk*   effuse—*to pour out*
yawp—*scream*   eddies—*small whirlpools*
scud—*a slight sudden shower or gust of wind*

Henry Wadsworth Longfellow

Edited by Frances Schoonmaker
Illustrated by Chad Wallace

HENRY WADSWORTH LONGFELLOW: "LET US, THEN, BE UP AND DOING"

When Henry Wadsworth Longfellow was born in 1807, Thomas Jefferson was President of the United States. Longfellow's family had been very involved in the American Revolution and in New England life and politics. The Longfellows were respected citizens of Portland, Maine, when skirmishes with the British started. In fact, the home of Henry's great-grandparents was burned by the British in October of 1775. His grandfather, Stephen, represented their district of Maine in the Massachusetts legislature and was a judge. In those days, Maine was not a separate state. His father, Stephen Longfellow, was a lawyer who had graduated from Harvard. He, too, served in the Massachusetts legislature and was elected to Congress.

Longfellow was named for his mother's brother, Henry Wadsworth, who died heroically in the Navy. Another uncle was a commodore in the Navy. The Wadsworth family was known for outstanding military service. Longfellow's grandfather, General Peleg Wadsworth brought together a company of minutemen and was later put in command of all the troops in eastern Maine during the Revolution. He was captured by the British and imprisoned in a fort. Along with another officer, General Wadsworth made a daring escape from prison. After the war, he, was elected to the Massachusetts legislature and later to Congress.

The Longfellows lived in town in a big, comfortable house that General Wadsworth had built. It was the first brick house in Portland. They had plenty, though they were not a wealthy family. The children took dancing lessons and Longfellow learned to play the piano and flute. His family is said to have had the first piano known in Portland. His parents, Stephen and Zilpah, had a small library and both of them enjoyed literature and encouraged their children to explore the family library and borrow books from the Portland library.

Many of Longfellow's poems are about childhood people and places. Because Portland was a seacoast town, the sea is the subject of many of his poems. In "The Wreck of the Hesperus," on page 21, Longfellow tells a tragic sea story. He wrote in his diary on December 30, 1839, that he had been sitting by the fire until midnight, "when suddenly it came into my mind to write 'The Ballad of the Schooner Hesperus'; which I accordingly did. Then I went to bed, but could not sleep. New thoughts were running in my mind, and I got up to add them to the ballad. It was three by the clock. I then went to bed and fell asleep." Longfellow often worked long into the night writing poetry.

As a boy, he loved to watch the blacksmith at work. He loved the "spreading chestnut tree" under which the blacksmith worked. Years later, in 1879, he tried to save the tree from being chopped down. But Portland city officials wanted to widen the street. Someone suggested that the tree be made into a chair for the poet. Public school children of Cambridge, Massachusetts, where Longfellow lived at the time, gave money for this project. The poet was known to love the company of children and go out of his way to be kind to them. He ordered that any child who wanted to see the chair they had given him should be allowed to do so. Many children came to see the chair — so many that the maids complained about having to wipe their fingerprints off the walls and furniture and their footprints off the floors.

In childhood days, he also watched the potter work at his wheel. To him it seemed to be magic that turned a lump of clay into a pot. In the poem "Turn, Turn," on page 16, Longfellow draws on his memories of the pottery and the mysterious wheel that seemed to sing along with the potter.

When Longfellow was fourteen, he began college. It was not uncommon for young men of his age to go to college. At fifteen, he and his brother, Stephen were allowed to live away from home and attend Bowdoin College in Brunswick. He began to be serious about writing poetry. By his junior year several of his poems had been published. One of his early poems is "Woods in Winter," on page 20. His college room looked out on a pine grove. But it is more likely that the young Longfellow was thinking of Deering's woods, a beautiful grove of oak on the outskirts of Portland. A hawthorn tree stood near the woods and under it was the pottery.

Longfellow's father wanted him to be a lawyer so that he could support himself. But young Henry was determined to be a writer, and a famous one! He wrote to his father, saying that he would be a lawyer in order to "support my *real* existence," as a writer. But something happened to change his father's mind. Longfellow was offered a position as professor in a new field of study at Bowdoin College: modern languages. He was even given money to spend three years in Europe learning the languages! So the eighteen-year-old Henry traveled to Europe to study in France, Spain, Italy, and Germany. He not only prepared himself to teach languages, but he followed his dream of studying literature. He was excited about studying languages. He wrote to one of his sisters, "by every language you learn, a new world is opened before you." Eventually he was able to read, write, and speak French, Italian, Spanish, and German. And he could read Swedish, Finnish, Danish, Norwegian, Dutch, and Portuguese!

When he returned home to begin his work, he married Mary Storer Potter. Mary had grown up in Portland, too. The couple lived in Brunswick for six years. Not only did he continue to write poetry, but he began to be known as an expert on languages. He was offered a position at Harvard as a professor of languages. To prepare for it, he and Mary spent another year in Europe where Longfellow worked to improve his German and studied Scandinavian literature. It was a sad time, however. Mary Longfellow was pregnant and had a miscarriage. She never fully recovered and died within a few weeks. Longfellow threw himself into his work, but he wrote in his diary, "At night I cry myself to sleep like a child."

Longfellow returned to Harvard in the fall of 1836. He taught and wrote for the next eighteen years. Many people of his day thought of him as a scholar and teacher, not as a poet. They used his books on language and literature. But others thought of him as a poet. Today, he is remembered for his poems.

After beginning his work at Harvard, Longfellow found rooms to rent in an old mansion in Cambridge, Massachusetts. It was a house with an interesting history. General Washington had used it as headquarters during the siege of Boston. There were lovely old elm trees in front and a garden behind. Little did he know that one day it would be given to him as a wedding present!

He fell in love with Frances Appleton, a young woman who liked him but did not want to marry him. When he asked her to marry him, "Fanny" turned him down. Longfellow was terribly hurt by this, but continued to be her friend. A few years later, she changed her mind, and they were married in the summer of 1843. His father-in-law, who was quite wealthy, bought the newlyweds the big house where Longfellow had rented rooms. There they were quite happy and entertained many friends in their home. One of their friends was Nathaniel Hawthorne, the famous author. They talked about writing a collection of fairy tales together. And Hawthorne passed along an idea to Longfellow that he used in his most famous poem, "Evangeline." The introduction to "Evangeline" is on page 34. It is a long narrative, or story poem. Hawthorne was very pleased with the poem that Longfellow had written and wrote about it in a New England newspaper. Another friend was Charles Sumner, probably Longfellow's best friend. Sumner was an outspoken abolitionist senator — that is to say, he opposed slavery. He made many enemies, even in the North.

Longfellow was not afraid to have outspoken friends. Nor was he afraid to stand up for what he believed. Once when he was on a ship, returning home from one of his trips abroad, he couldn't sleep. He kept thinking about the Africans who had been stolen from their homes and put in ships to be taken to the United States and sold as slaves. He began to compose a set of eight poems which were published in a little book called *Poems on Slavery*. It took courage to publish them. Longfellow made many enemies by doing so. "The Witnesses," tells about slaves who died when their slave ships were lost at sea (see page 28). "The Slave's Dream" is about a slave who remembers his life in Africa (see page 29). When the Civil War broke out, Longfellow was deeply troubled that the nation had been unable to settle the question of slavery without a war. He wrote the carol, "Christmas Bells," which is on page 31. It is still a popular carol, but two of the verses do not appear with the carol in modern carol books.

For nearly twenty years, the Longfellows were happily settled. They had three daughters and two sons. One of the poems in a famous collection, *Tales of a Wayside Inn,* tells of his affection for his daughters. "The Children's Hour," is on page 40. In this book, Longfellow imagines a group of people meeting at an inn and each telling a story. Each of the stories is interesting to read, but the most famous is "Paul Revere's Ride." On page 43 you can find the first half of the story. This is the part that some people who study Longfellow believe to be the complete part of the poem. The rest was somewhat unfinished and based more on imagination than on facts. So many people have read the poem and loved it that they believe it is the actual history of what happened. But it is actually Longellow's imagination building on a real event.

There are people who think that Longfellow's life was too easy for him to be a real poet. It is true that he lived a comfortable life. But his life was not as easy as it might seem. It took him many years to find his voice as a poet (that is, what he had to say through poetry that would be really unique). And he could not give writing poetry his full attention. He wanted to be a good teacher and continued to write about language and literature. He never got over the death of his first wife and their baby. He knew what it was like to be rejected when Fanny refused to marry him. And, after they had been married for nearly twenty years, she was died in an terrible accident. She was sealing a letter with a candle when her gown caught fire. Longfellow heard her screaming and came running from a nearby room. He grabbed her in his arms and put out the flames, but it was too late. She died from the burns, suffering great pain. Longfellow had serious burns, too. He grieved for her the rest of his life.

He spent his last months by the sea with one of his daughters and her family. He died March 14, 1882. But up until he died, Longfellow kept writing. After he published "A Psalm of Life" (page 36) and a book of poems, *Voices of the Night,* he became a real celebrity. "Hymn to the Night" is also from this book. When *The Song of Hiawatha* was published, people were most eager to read it. It became a favorite. In this poem, Longfellow tells about all of Hiawatha's life. (A section from "Hiawatha's Childhood," is on page 37.) His poetry was just as popular in Europe. People looked for his work, read it, and talked about it. Some of his best loved poems were not his best writing. But people memorized them and used them in their everyday talk about life. As you read his poems, you may notice some lines that seem familiar. That is because people are still using his words in their talk about everyday life, even when they don't know they are quoting Longfellow. Maybe you have heard someone say, "Into each life some rain must fall." This expression comes from "The Rainy Day," on page 12. Or, perhaps you have heard people say they want to leave "footprints on the sands of time." This expression is from "A Psalm of Life," on page 36. Henry Wadsworth Longfellow left many "footprints on the sands of time." They are the poems that we can still enjoy today.

THE ARROW AND THE SONG

I shot an arrow into the air,
It fell to earth, I knew not where;
For, so swiftly it flew, the sight
Could not follow it in its flight.

I breathed a song into the air,
It fell to earth, I knew not where;
For who has sight so keen and strong,
That it can follow the flight of song?

Long, long afterward, in an oak
I found the arrow, still unbroke;
And the song, from beginning to end,
I found again in the heart of a friend.

FOUR BY THE CLOCK

Four by the clock! And yet not day;
But the great world rolls and wheels away,
With its cities on land, and its ships at sea,
Into the dawn that is to be!

Only the lamp in the anchored bark
Sends its glimmer across the dark,
And the heavy breathing of the sea
Is the only sound that comes to me.

bark - *a boat*

DAYBREAK

A wind came up out of the sea,
And said, "O mists, make room for me."

It hailed the ships, and cried, "Sail on,
Ye mariners, the night is gone."

And hurried landward far away,
Crying, "Awake! it is the day."

It said unto the forest, "Shout!
Hang all your leafy banners out!"

It touched the wood-bird's folded wing,
And said, "O bird, awake and sing."

And o'er the farms, "O chanticleer,
Your clarion blow; the day is near."

It whispered to the fields of corn,
"Bow down, and hail the coming morn."

It shouted through the belfry-tower,
"Awake, O bell! proclaim the hour."

It crossed the churchyard with a sigh,
And said, "Not yet! in quiet lie."*

chanticleer—*a rooster*
clarion—*a shrill-sounding trumpet*

Some people believe that all the dead who are buried in graves and churchyards will come to life at the end of time.

THE RAINY DAY

The day is cold, and dark, and dreary;
It rains, and the wind is never weary;
The vine still clings to the mouldering wall,
But at every gust the dead leaves fall,
And the day is dark and dreary.

My life is cold, and dark, and dreary;
It rains, and the wind is never weary;
My thoughts still cling to the mouldering Past,
But the hopes of youth fall thick in the blast,
And the days are dark and dreary.

Be still, sad heart! And cease repining;
Behind the clouds is the sun still shining;
Thy fate is the common fate of all,
Into each life some rain must fall,
Some days must be dark and dreary.

mouldering—*moldy or overgrown with mold*
repining—*feeling unhappy or discontented*

The Village Blacksmith

Under a spreading chestnut-tree
    The village smithy stands;
The smith, a mighty man is he,
    With large and sinewy hands;
And the muscles of his brawny arms
    Are strong as iron bands.

His hair is crisp, and black, and long,
    His face is like the tan;
His brow is wet with honest sweat,
    He earns whate'er he can,
And looks the whole world in the face,
    For he owes not any man.

Week in, week out, from morn till night,
    You can hear his bellows blow;
You can hear him swing his heavy sledge,
    With measured beat and slow,
Like a sexton ringing the village bell,
    When the evening sun is low.

And children coming home from school
    Look in at the open door;
They love to see the flaming forge,
    And hear the bellows roar,
And catch the burning sparks that fly
    Like chaff from a threshing-floor.

He goes on Sunday to the church,
    And sits among his boys;
He hears the parson pray and preach,
    He hears his daughter's voice,
Singing in the village choir,
    And it makes his heart rejoice.

It sounds to him like her mother's voice,
　　Singing in Paradise!
He needs must think of her once more
　　How in the grave she lies;
And with his hard, rough hand he wipes
　　A tear out of his eyes.

Toiling,—rejoicing,—sorrowing,
　　Onward through life he goes;
Each morning sees some task begin,
　　Each evening sees it close;
Something attempted, something done,
　　Has earned a night's repose.

Thanks, thanks to thee, my worthy friend,
　　For the lesson thou hast taught!
Thus at the flaming forge of life
　　Our fortunes must be wrought;
Thus on its sounding anvil shaped
　　Each burning deed and thought.

sinewy—— *strong, tough*

bellows—*A tool the blacksmith uses to pump air on a fire
　　to make it hotter.*

sexton—— *One who rings the church bells. Sometimes the
　　sexton is the one who helps care for the church.*

chaff—*the husks that grow on grain that are separated by
　　threshing*

anvil—*the smith uses an anvil, or block of iron, to put his
　　work on when he is shaping it*

TURN, TURN, MY WHEEL*

Turn, turn, my wheel! Turn round and round
Without a pause, without a sound:
    So spins the flying world away!
This clay, well mixed with marl and sand,
Follows the motion of my hand;
For some must follow, and some command,
    Though all are made of clay!

Thus sang the Potter at his task
Beneath the blossoming hawthorn-tree,
While o'er his features, like a mask,
The quilted sunshine and leaf-shade
Moved, as the boughs above him swayed,
And clothed him, till he seemed to be
A figure woven in tapestry,
So sumptuously was he arrayed
In that magnificent attire
Of sable tissue flaked with fire.
Like a magician he appeared,
A conjurer without book or beard;
And while he plied his magic art—
For it was magical to me—
I stood in silence and apart,
And wondered more and more to see
That shapeless, lifeless mass of clay
Rise up to meet the master's hand,
And now contract and now expand,
And even his slightest touch obey.

*"Turn, Turn, My Wheel" is from a much longer poem, "Keramos."

marl—a red-colored clay soil
sumptuously—costly and magnificently decorated

AFTERMATH

When the summer fields are mown,
When the birds are fledged and flown,
    And the dry leaves strew the path;
With the falling of the snow,
With the cawing of the crow,
Once again the fields we mow
    And gather in the aftermath.

Not the sweet, new grass with flowers
Is this harvesting of ours;
    Not the upland clover bloom;
But the rowen mixed with weeds,
Tangled tufts from marsh and meads,
Where the poppy drops its seeds
    In the silence and the gloom.

fledged—*a young bird that is grown with all its feathers*
rowen—*the second growth of a crop of hay or grass during the growing season; it is
    also known as aftermath, the title Longfellow chose for the poem.*
meads—*meadows, fields*

HAUNTED HOUSES*

All houses wherein men have lived and died
　　Are haunted houses. Through the open doors
The harmless phantoms on their errands glide,
　　With feet that make no sound upon the floors.

We meet them at the doorway, on the stair,
　　Along the passages they come and go,
Impalpable impressions on the air,
　　A sense of something moving to and fro.

There are more guests at the table than the hosts
　　Invited; the illuminated hall
Is thronged with quiet, inoffensive ghosts,
　　As silent as the pictures on the wall.

The stranger at my fireside cannot see
　　The forms I see, nor hear the sounds I hear;
He but perceives what is; while unto me
　　All that has been is visible and clear.

*These are the beginning stanzas of a longer poem in which
Longfellow thinks about how our lives are connected to those
who have lived and died before us.*

254

WOODS IN WINTER

When winter winds are piercing chill,
    And through the hawthorn blows the gale,
With solemn feet I tread the hill,
    That overbrows the lonely vale.

O'er the bare upland, and away
    Through the long reach of desert woods,
The embracing sunbeams chastely play,
    And gladden these deep solitudes.

Where, twisted round the barren oak,
    The summer vine in beauty clung,
And summer winds the stillness broke,
    The crystal icicle is hung.

Where, from their frozen urns, mute springs
    Pour out the river's gradual tide,
Shrilly the skater's iron rings,
    And voices fill the wooden side.

Alas! How changed from the fair scene,
    When birds sang out their mellow lay,
And winds were soft, and woods were green,
    And the song ceased not with the day!

But still wild music is abroad,
    Pale, desert woods! within your crowd;
And gathering winds, in hoarse accord,
    Amid the vocal reeds pipe loud.

Chill airs and wintry winds! my ear
    Has grown familiar with your song;
I hear it in the opening year,
    I listen, and it cheers me long.

chastely—*innocently, purely*

THE WRECK OF THE HESPERUS

It was the schooner Hesperus,
　　That sailed the wintry sea;
And skipper had taken his little daughter,
　　To bear him company.

Blue were her eyes as the fairy-flax,
　　Her cheeks like the dawn of day,
And her bosom white as the hawthorn buds,
　　That ope in the month of May.

The skipper he stood beside the helm,
　　His pipe was in his mouth,
And he watched how the veering flaw did blow
　　The smoke now West, now South.

Then up and spake an old Sailor,
　　Had sailed to the Spanish Main,
"I pray thee, put into yonder port,
　　For I fear a hurricane.

"Last night, the moon had a golden ring,
　　And to-night no moon we see!"
The skipper, he blew a whiff from his pipe,
　　And a scornful laugh laughed he.

Colder and louder blew the wind,
　　A gale from the Northeast,
The snow fell hissing in the brine,
　　And the billows frothed like yeast.

Down came the storm, and smote amain
　　The vessel in its strength;
She shuddered and paused, like a frightened steed,
　　Then leaped her cable's length.

"Come hither! Come hither! My little daughter,
    And do not tremble so;
For I can weather the roughest gale
    That ever wind did blow."

He wrapped her warm in his seaman's coat
    And against the stinging blast;
He cut a rope from a broken spar,
    And bound her to the mast.

"O father! I hear the church-bells ring,
    Oh say, what may it be?"
"'T is a fog-bell on a rock-bound coast!"—
    And he steered for the open sea.

"O father! I hear the sound of guns,
    Oh say, what may it be?"
"Some ship in distress, that cannot live
    In such an angry sea!"

"O father! I see a gleaming light,
    Oh say, what may it be?"
But the father answered never a word,
    A frozen corpse was he.

Lashed to the helm, all stiff and stark,
    With his face turned to the skies,
The lantern gleamed through the gleaming snow
    On his fixed and glassy eyes.

Then the maiden clasped her hands and prayed
    That saved she might be;
And she thought of Christ, who stilled the wave,
    On the Lake of Galilee.

And fast through the midnight dark and drear,
    Through the whistling sleet and snow,
Like a sheeted ghost, the vessel swept
    Tow'rds the reef of Norman's Woe.

And ever the fitful gusts between
    A sound came from the land;
It was the sound of the trampling surf
    On the rocks and the hard sea-sand.

The breakers were right beneath her bows,
    She drifted a dreary wreck,
And a whooping billow swept the crew
    Like icicles from her deck.

She struck where the white and fleecy waves
    Looked soft as carded wool,
But the cruel rocks, they gored her side
    Like the horns of an angry bull.

Her rattling shrouds, all sheathed in ice,
    With the masts went by the board;
Like a vessel of glass, she strove and sank,
    Ho! Ho! The breakers roared!

At daybreak on the bleak sea-beach,
    A fisherman stood aghast,
To see the form of a maiden fair,
    Lashed close to a drifting mast.

The salt sea was frozen on her breast,
    The salt tears in her eyes;
And he saw her hair, like the brown sea-weed,
    On the billows fall and rise.

Such was the wreck of the Hesperus,
    In the midnight and the snow!
Christ save us all from a death like this,
    On the reef of Norman's Woe!

ope—*open*

flaw—*a sudden gust of wind, often with rain or snow*

amain—*forcefully, and at great speed*

carded wool—*wool fiber that has been combed into thread*
   with a wire brush

THE SOUND OF THE SEA

The sea awoke at midnight from its sleep,
    And round the pebbly beaches far and wide
    I heard the first wave of the rising tide
Rush onward with uninterrupted sweep;

A voice out of the silence of the deep,
    A sound mysteriously multiplied
    As of a cataract from the mountain's side,
Or roar of winds upon a wooded steep.

So comes to us at times, from the unknown
    And inaccessible solitudes of being,
    The rushing of the sea-tides of the soul;

And inspirations, that we deem our own,
    Are some divine foreshadowing and foreseeing
    Of things beyond our reason or control.

cataract—*waterfall*

BECALMED

Becalmed upon the sea of Thought,
Still unattained the land it sought,
My mind, with loosely-hanging sails,
Lies waiting the auspicious gales.

On either side, behind, before,
The ocean stretches like a floor,—
A level floor of amethyst,
Crowned by a golden dome of mist.

Blow, breath of inspiration, blow!
Shake and uplift this golden glow!
And fill the canvas of the mind
With wafts of thy celestial wind.

Blow, breath of song! until I feel
The straining sail, the lifting keel,
The life of the awakening sea,
Its motion and its mystery!

auspicious—*favorable*
amethyst—*a precious stone of blue-violet or purple*
celestial—*heavenly*

THE TIDE RISES, THE TIDE FALLS

The tide rises, the tide falls,
The twilight darkens, the curlew calls;
Along the sea-sands damp and brown
The traveller hastens toward the town,
    And the tide rises, the tide falls.

Darkness settles on roofs and walls,
But the sea, the sea in the darkness calls;
The little waves, with their soft, white hands,
Efface the footprints in the sands,
    And the tide rises, the tide falls.

The morning breaks; the steeds in their stalls
Stamp and neigh, as the hostler calls;
The day returns, but nevermore
Returns the traveller to the shore,
    And the tide rises, the tide falls.

curlew—*a large brown wading bird with long legs*
hostler—*stableman; groom*

THE WITNESSES

In Ocean's wide domains,
    Half buried in the sands,
Lie skeletons in chains,
    With shackled feet and hands.

Beyond the fall of dews,
    Deeper than plummet lies,
Float ships, with all their crews,
    No more to sink nor rise.

There the black Slave-ship swims,
    Freighted with human forms,
Whose fettered, fleshless limbs
    Are not the sport of storms.

These are the bones of Slaves;
    They gleam from the abyss;
They cry, from yawning waves,
    "We are the Witnesses!"

Within Earth's wide domains
    Are markets for men's lives;
Their necks are galled with chains,
    Their wrists are cramped with gyves.

Dead bodies, that the kite
    In deserts makes its prey;
Murders, that with affright
    Scare school-boys from their play!

All evil thoughts and deeds;
    Anger, and lust, and pride;
The foulest, rankest weeds,
    That choke Life's groaning tide!

These are the woes of Slaves;
    They glare from the abyss;
They cry, from unknown graves,
    "We are the Witnesses!"

gyves—*shackles*
plummet—*a heavy weight used by builders to keep walls*
    in a straight line. It also means to weigh down, like a
    dead weight.
fettered—*chained;shackled*
galled—*sore and irritated*
kite—*bird of prey like the*
    hawk or falcon

THE SLAVE'S DREAM

Beside the ungathered rice he lay,
 His sickle in his hand;
His breast was bare, his matted hair
 Was buried in the sand.
Again, in the mist and shadow of sleep,
 He saw his Native land.

Wide through the landscape of his dreams
 The lordly Niger flowed;
Beneath the palm-trees on the plain
 Once more a king he strode;
And heard the tinkling caravans
 Descend the mountain road.

He saw once more his dark-eyed queen
 Among her children stand;
They clasped his neck, they kissed his cheeks,
 They held him by the hand!—
A tear burst from the sleeper's lids
 And fell into the sand.

And then at furious speed he rode
 Along the Niger's bank;
His bridle-reins were golden chains,
 And, with a martial clank,
At each leap he could feel his scabbard of steel
 Smiting his stallion's flank.

Before him, like a blood-red flag,
 The bright flamingoes flew;
From morn till night he followed their flight,
 O'er plains where the tamarind grew,
Till he saw the roofs of Caffre huts,
 And the ocean rose to view.

At night he heard the lion roar,
 And the hyena scream,

And the river-horse, as he crushed the reeds
 Beside some hidden stream;
And it passed, like a glorious roll of drums,
 Through the triumph of his dream.

The forests with their myriad tongues,
 Shouted of liberty;
And the Blast of the Desert cried aloud,
 With a voice so wild and free,
That he started in his sleep and smiled
 At their tempestuous glee.

He did not feel the driver's whip,
 Nor the burning heat of day;
For Death had illumined the Land of Sleep,
 And his lifeless body lay
A worn-out fetter, that the soul
 Had broken and thrown away!

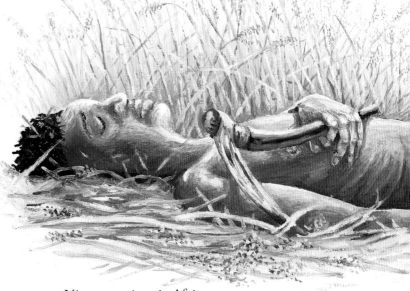

Niger—a river in Africa
scabbard—the case that protects the blade of a
 sword
tamarind—a tropical tree with yellow flowers
Caffre—a South African from the Bantu people
river-horse—the hippopotamus
myriad—a countless number of things

265

FRAGMENTS

December 18, 1847

Soft through the silent air descend the feathery snow-flakes;
White are the distant hills, white are the neighboring fields;
Only the marshes are brown, and the river rolling among them
Weareth the leaden hue seen in the eyes of the blind.

SNOW-FLAKES

Out of the bosom of the air,
 Out of the cloud-folds of her garments shaken,
Over the woodlands brown and bare,
 Over the harvest-fields forsaken,
Silent, and soft, and slow
Descends the snow.

Even as our cloudy fancies take
 Suddenly shape in some divine expression,
Even as the troubled heart doth make
 In the white countenance confession,
The troubled sky reveals
The grief it feels.

This is the poem of the air,
 Slowly in silent syllables recorded;
This the secret of despair,
 Long in its cloudy bosom hoarded,
Now whispered and revealed
To wood and field.

countenance—*appearance, expression on the face*

CHRISTMAS BELLS*

I heard the bells on Christmas Day
Their old, familiar carols play,
And wild and sweet
The words repeat
Of peace on earth, good-will to men!

And thought how, as the day had come,
The belfries of all Christendom
Had rolled along
The unbroken song
Of peace on earth, good-will to men!

Till, ringing, singing on its way,
The world revolved from night to day,
A voice, a chime,
A chant sublime
Of peace on earth, good-will to men!

Then from each black, accursed mouth
The cannon thundered in the South,
And with the sound
The carols drowned
Of peace on earth, good-will to men!

It was as if an earthquake rent
The hearth-stones of a continent,
And made forlorn
The households born
Of peace on earth, good-will to men!

And in despair I bowed my head;
"There is no peace on earth," I said;
"For hate is strong,
And mocks the song
Of peace on earth, good-will to men!"

Then pealed the bells more loud and deep:
"God is not dead; nor doth he sleep!
The Wrong shall fail,
The Right prevail,
With peace on earth, good-will to men!"

*The Civil War in the United States took place between 1861 and 1865. This poem was written in 1864.

267

AFTERNOON IN FEBRUARY

The day is ending,
The night is descending;
The marsh is frozen,
The river dead.

Through clouds like ashes
The red sun flashes
On village windows
That glimmer red.

The snow recommences;
The buried fences
Mark no longer
The road o'er the plain;

While through the meadows
Like fearful shadows,
Slowly passes
A funeral train.

The bell is pealing,
And every feeling
Within me responds
To the dismal knell;

Shadows are trailing,
My heart is bewailing
And tolling within
Like a funeral bell.

HAROUN AL RASCHID

One day, Haroun Al Raschid read
A book wherein the poet said:—

"Where are the kings, and where the rest
Of those who once the world possessed?

"They're gone with all their pomp and show,
They're gone the way that thou shalt go.

"O thou who choosest for thy share
The world, and what the world calls fair,

"Take all that it can give or lend,
But know that death is at the end!"

Haroun Al Raschid bowed his head:
Tears fell upon the page he read.

THE FOREST PRIMEVAL*

This is the forest primeval. The murmuring pines and the hemlocks,
Bearded with moss, and in garments green, indistinct in the twilight,
Stand like Druids of eld, with voices sad and prophetic,
Stand like harpers hoar, with beards that rest on their bosoms.
Loud from its rocky caverns, the deep-voiced neighboring ocean
Speaks, and in accents disconsolate answers the wail of the forest.

*This is the introduction to the long narrative (story) poem, "Evangeline."

eld—old

harpers hoar—hoar means greyish-white; here Longfellow probably intends it to
   mean hoar hair, or gray hair to go with the harper's long beard. The harper is a
   person who plays a harp.